Praise for *Breakthrough!*

This book will set off enough light bulbs to make your brain look like a Christmas tree. You will be giving away copies.

JIM WILDER
Author and neurotheologian

Marcus is the son of spiritual giants who were trailblazers that passed the torch so he could lead the way for people to find hope, healing, deliverance, and joy. Marcus has run full speed ahead and given us a brilliant book! In *Breakthrough!*, Marcus has taken a lifetime of study, observation, experience, and practice then woven it into one marvelous project. *Breakthrough!* is the book our world needs! Marcus shares profound stories of life-change that captivate the reader. *Breakthrough!* is a journey that includes antidotes and insights with wisdom, expertise, brain science, Scripture, and transformation to cast a vision of what's possible for a life that is full and abundant in Christ. You will love this book! You will want to share this with everyone you know. You will gain a captivating road map that details true essentials for lasting change. Our families and communities need *Breakthrough!* so we can develop ways to grow, heal, mature, and become the people God created us to be. We can learn to express this life with depth and clarity in ways that draw others to the living God.

CHRIS M. COURSEY
President of THRIVEtoday; author of *The Joy Switch*

What a treasury of wisdom and insights as Marcus shares the things he has learned over the decades of working with people in pain. His solid biblical worldview and unique ability to make the complex simple makes this book accessible to anyone. Thank you, Marcus.

ALAINE PAKKALA
Lydia Discipleship Ministries

Breakthrough! is a great read for anyone who is ministering to God's hurting people and also helpful for those looking for support. Marcus takes the lid off a number of counseling models and shares their strengths and weaknesses along with how to employ them wisely to bring freedom to many. He is spot on when clarifying that one method does not fit all situations. He doesn't offer a simple formula but a toolbox of skills to help hurting people get around the roadblocks that hinder them from connecting to God and to others around them. Marcus once more takes complicated concepts and presents them in an easy-to-understand way. Whether you are a student learning about counseling or have been practicing for over twenty years, there are nuggets of truth here that will enrich your ministry.

BOB HARDIN
Director, Northwest Biblical Counseling Center

It's always refreshing for me to find a book on personal growth that gets out of the shallows of symptom reduction and addresses the goal of all good therapeutic work: developing maturity. In *Breakthrough!*, Marcus Warner leads us on a journey toward maturity that aligns with God's goal for all who love Him—to make us more like Jesus (Rom. 8:28–29).

DAN RUMBERGER
Clinical Psychologist

What do people do when they are "stuck" in life or in their walk of faith, fight discouragement and defeat, face overwhelming obstacles in seeking the right solutions . . . and wonder how to hear God's voice in the middle of it all? They often look for the right pathway to guide the journey. Psalm 119:105 tells us that God's Word is a lamp to our feet and a light to our path. What an encouraging metaphor to describe *Breakthrough!* by Marcus Warner. The pages and chapters provide a biblical and practical compass and road map for Christ followers to find their way.

ERIC SCALISE
Senior Vice President and Chief Strategy Officer, Hope for the Heart

BREAK-THROUGH!

5

ESSENTIAL STRATEGIES FOR FREEDOM, HEALING, AND WHOLENESS

MARCUS WARNER

MOODY PUBLISHERS

CHICAGO

All Scripture quotations, unless otherwise indicated, are taken from the Holy Bible, New International Version®, NIV®. Copyright ©1973, 1978, 1984, 2011 by Biblica, Inc.™ Used by permission of Zondervan. All rights reserved worldwide. www.zondervan.com The "NIV" and "New International Version" are trademarks registered in the United States Patent and Trademark Office by Biblica, Inc.™

Scripture quotations marked (esv) are from the ESV® Bible (The Holy Bible, English Standard Version®), © 2001 by Crossway, a publishing ministry of Good News Publishers. Used by permission. All rights reserved. The ESV text may not be quoted in any publication made available to the public by a Creative Commons license. The ESV may not be translated in whole or in part into any other language.

Scripture quotations marked csb have been taken from the Christian Standard Bible®, Copyright © 2017 by Holman Bible Publishers. Used by permission. Christian Standard Bible® and CSB are federally registered trademarks of Holman Bible Publishers.

Names and details of some stories have been changed to protect the privacy of individuals.

Edited by Ashleigh Slater
Interior design: Ragont Design
Cover design: Thinkpen Design
Cover graphic of hiker copyright © 2023 by art GALA/Shutterstock (1897547908). All rights reserved.
Cover graphic of mountains copyright © 2023 by patrimony designs ltd/Shutterstock (1914449332). All rights reserved.
Cover graphic of celebrating hiker copyright © Jemastock/Shutterstock (1986674341). All rights reserved.
Author photo: Jenn Fike

Library of Congress Cataloging-in-Publication Data

Names: Warner, Marcus, author.
Title: Breakthrough : 5 essential strategies for freedom, healing, and wholeness / Marcus Warner.
Description: Chicago : Moody Publishers, [2024] | Includes bibliographical references. | Summary: "Breakthrough! takes the Bible and brain science-with the Holy Spirit-and provides an integrative approach to building emotional resilience. Our memories and hearts can heal. We can mature and grow in Christ. Whether you're at your end or simply in need of some spiritual vivacity, this book won't disappoint"-- Provided by publisher.
Identifiers: LCCN 2023039255 (print) | LCCN 2023039256 (ebook) | ISBN 9780802431745 (paperback) | ISBN 9780802473042 (ebook)
Subjects: LCSH: Emotions--Religious aspects--Christianity. | Emotional maturity--Religious aspects--Christianity. | Emotions--Biblical teaching. | BISAC: RELIGION / Christian Ministry / Counseling & Recovery | RELIGION / Christian Living / Spiritual Growth
Classification: LCC BV4597.3 .W36 2024 (print) | LCC BV4597.3 (ebook) | DDC 248.4--dc23/eng/20231016
LC record available at https://lccn.loc.gov/2023039255
LC ebook record available at https://lccn.loc.gov/2023039256

Originally delivered by fleets of horse-drawn wagons, the affordable paperbacks from D. L. Moody's publishing house resourced the church and served everyday people. Now, after more than 125 years of publishing and ministry, Moody Publishers' mission remains the same—even if our delivery systems have changed a bit. For more information on other books (and resources) created from a biblical perspective, go to www.moodypublishers.com or write to:

Moody Publishers
820 N. LaSalle Boulevard
Chicago, IL 60610

1 3 5 7 9 10 8 6 4 2

Printed in the United States of America

This book is dedicated to my mother, Eleanor Warner,
who spent most of her "empty nester" years helping women
find freedom and grow in their walk with God.
She loved to see people experience the breakthrough they
needed in the struggles they faced.

CONTENTS

FOREWORD

OVER THE PAST 30+ YEARS, I've had the privilege of walking beside countless people during *Hope in the Night*, our live call-in counseling radio program. I've talked with strugglers about their life stories. I've seen the helpless receive help and the hopeless find hope. In their voices, I hear how the compassion of Christ breaks through their anger and fear. I hear how the love of the Lord breaks through their trauma and pain to redeem and restore their lives. In the end, that is what this book is all about—relieving pain, repairing damage, and rebuilding lives.

The Hebrew word for breakthrough, *peres*, means a "gap" or "break," which can also refer to a gap in an enemy's wall. It calls to mind the spiritual battles we face and the enemy of our soul who seeks "to steal and kill and destroy" (John 10:10). Satan, who is called the "father of lies" (8:44), delights in defeating Christians. Yet we can breakthrough his walls because we have a Savior who is far greater (1 John 4:4).

At times, we've all needed to change. And we've all needed help. With God's help and a willing heart, anyone can change. There are no hopeless situations. "The God of all grace" (1 Peter 5:10) can cause a breakthrough and mend the broken heart. He is in the life-changing business, and one way He changes our lives is by changing our thinking.

During WWII, no one was more respected as a military genius than American general George Patton. Likewise, no one was more feared than his archenemy, the German field marshal Erwin Rommel. His clever tactics earned him the nickname "The Desert Fox." Rommel's military successes were renowned, yet Patton lured him into a trap that resulted in defeat of the German troops. Ultimately, Patton outfoxed The Fox! This major shift in the war led to the ultimate allied victory over Nazi Germany.

What prepared Patton to defeat his cunning enemy? In the movie *Patton*, when Rommel asked, Patton answered, "I read your book!" He had studied the warfare tactics of his enemy. In the same way, as believers, we need to study the strategies used by our unseen enemy, Satan. We need to unmask his lies, and his tactics. How many of Satan's lies do we struggle with?

When I first met Marcus at a convention dinner, I walked away surprised at the range of topics we covered in our hour-long conversation. Most Christians, even most Christian leaders, know little about subjects like spiritual warfare, the occult, and satanic ritual abuse. Yet Marcus has immense experience engaging in the strategic battle to help men and women win the spiritual war that they don't even know has a name. I thank God for Marcus Warner—a needed voice for today.

I have participated in many deliverance sessions—always with one or two other praying Christians present. I remember a Christian woman telling me there was block in her life, something she couldn't get over. So, on a Sunday afternoon at 3:00 p.m., three of us met with her. After prayer, we began with our inventory of her involvement in the occult. Periodically, she could not get the words out. I suggested singing a Christian song. "No! No!" she objected. "I can't handle Christian music." So, we let the idea of music go.

Three different times during our twelve hours together she looked like she was in pain, clutching her stomach. I prayed, "If there is a demonic influence attacking her body, in the name of the Lord Jesus Christ and by the power of the Holy Spirit, I command that you release her body from attack and be gone from her body." And sure enough, each time she straightened up—pain free. Breakthrough!

She shared that she had been unable to go to church for years but couldn't understand why. We prayed for her block. Finally, she had memories of her mother, as a Sunday school teacher taking her to church earlier than others. She was a young girl by herself, but a man multiple times found her alone and he sexually abused her. Memory breakthrough!

Eventually, we concluded at 3:00 in the morning. All of a sudden, she exclaimed with a big smile, "Let's sing *Heavenly Sunshine!*" I grabbed a hymn book, and we all sang the song together.

The second verse gave me chills:

"Shadows around me, shadows above me.
Never conceal my Savior and Guide;
He is the light, in Him is no darkness;
Ever I'm walking close to His side."

She had no problem singing every verse. Breakthrough!

From that point on she had no problem going to any church. Breakthrough! Breakthrough!

At times, strugglers feel they cannot overcome their past, and especially their current challenges. However, the Bible says, "Everyone who has been born of God overcomes the world. And this is the victory that has overcome the world—our faith. Who is it that overcomes the world except the one who believes that Jesus is the Son of God?" (1 John 5:4–5 ESV).

Faith means taking God at His word. If God said it, that settles it!

This acrostic on Faith focuses on the object our faith:

Focus on Christ as God, the Son,
Acknowledge that He has overcome the world,
Identify with Jesus, knowing His victory is our victory,
Trust in the absolute truth of God's Word, and

Hold up His Word as our measuring rod against the world's standards.

By exercising faith, we are able to exchange wrong beliefs with right beliefs. We can experience greater joy in our daily walk with Christ, have more balanced emotions, and to hear the Holy Spirit's counsel, and to move into greater maturity.

Marcus Warner has written a masterful book on the process of transformation. He underscores our need for emotional regulation, the vital role of our brain in personal development, the essential impact of us having right beliefs, and how to be led by the Spirit of God. All of these areas create the right pathway that leads to needed breakthroughs, and to ultimately achieve true maturity in Christ.

Beginning with the very first chapter, I invite you to discover how you can experience an authentic breakthrough to all God has for you—then become the person He created you to be. Nothing could be more fulfilling!

JUNE HUNT
Founder & CSO (Chief Servant Officer), Hope for the Heart and the Hope Center
Author, *Seeing Yourself Through God's Eyes*

MY STORY

I STARTED TEACHING Old Testament and systematic theology at a Christian college when I was twenty-five years old, and I loved it. I fully expected to stay in the academic arena my entire career. But there was another side of ministry running parallel to the academics, and that was my involvement with spiritual warfare and emotional healing. I never hung out a shingle, but once word spreads that you are willing to deal with some of these issues, people find you.

My mom and dad were known for their biblically balanced approach to spiritual warfare and routinely met with people who were looking for some kind of breakthrough. My father taught courses on spiritual warfare at Trinity Evangelical Divinity School and wrote two books on the topic. The first book, *Spiritual Warfare*, was based on a series of lectures he did at Fuller Seminary.[1] His second book was coauthored with Dr. Neil T. Anderson and is still available as *The Essential Guide to Spiritual Warfare*.[2]

Between the ages of sixty-five and eighty-five, my mother, Eleanor Warner, met with over four hundred young women to mentor them. She usually met with them for at least ten weeks. She would help them explore their identity in Christ and walk them through Neil Anderson's *Steps to Freedom in Christ*. The transformation these women generally experienced was amazing. When my mom passed away at age eighty-five, the funeral was filled with grateful women who had stories to tell of how their lives had been changed.

A DEMONIC ENCOUNTER

While I was in seminary, I began to sit in on sessions with my parents. One night, we went to visit a lady from a nearby church. Her suburban home was lovely. It was nicely decorated, and everything was orderly. She brought us some cookies and tea before we started. There was nothing in the environment to suggest that she had any profound issues.

At that point in their ministry, my parents tended to get called when someone suspected demonic activity. This was no different. My dad opened with a prayer designed to "tick off" any demons present. He prayed about Christ's victory at the cross and how every knee would bow and how the destiny of Christ's foes was the lake of fire, and how this woman belonged to Jesus. Well, the prayer got a reaction. Before I realized what was happening, the woman started rolling around on the floor and growling. My parents both began binding the demons and started walking this woman through a process that ended with her rejoicing at the amazing breakthrough she had experienced.

Sessions like this started happening more often. At first, I mostly watched. Soon, I started helping. Before long, they let me run the sessions. Around this time, my father left his position at Trinity and joined Neil T. Anderson as the International Director of Freedom in Christ Ministries. Soon, I found myself meeting with someone almost every week who wanted to go through the *Steps to Freedom in Christ*.

By the time I was in my mid-thirties, I had met with hundreds of people who were dealing with some serious issues. Some had been deeply wounded as children, most had sexual trauma, many had addictions, and nearly all of them were battling some level of emotional distress.

Over the next ten years, I found myself swimming in the deep end of the pool, spending much of my time ministering to people who had been clinically diagnosed with dissociative identity disorder and all of the trauma and dysfunction that produces such issues.[3] A lot of my time went into pastoral care.

COLLECTING TOOLS

Along the way, I began collecting tools for helping the people we ministered to. We always used the Bible, we always taught people their identity in Christ, and we routinely dealt with demonic issues. But more and more often, we began to help people learn how to connect with God through listening prayer or what some call conversational prayer, especially when it came to dealing with wounds from the past. Some of the sessions felt like having a front-row seat to the miraculous. We saw one woman transform from someone who hated God and despised Christianity into a person who loved Jesus and started writing worship songs about Him. First, she learned to trust the people in the group and eventually built enough confidence in the group that she was willing to take a chance on listening prayer. I remember her first prayer went something like this, "God, You know I hate You. But these people seem legit, so I am willing to give You a chance. If You want to do something to heal the wounds in my past, I'm okay with that." A few hours later, she was singing praises to her new best friend.

As a pastor, I spent, on average, about eight hours every week meeting with hurting people. I gradually developed a system for trying to get the most out of a two-hour session by focusing on root issues, listening prayer, and spiritual warfare. I saw a lot of people experience some level of breakthrough in those days—not because I was an amazing counselor, but because God always showed up.

After seven years as a pastor, I suddenly found myself at a crossroads. The church leaders told me they believed God had a national ministry for me and that I needed a push out of the nest to get started.

However, that meant I was suddenly not the pastor of the church. It had a big impact on my family, and I found myself wondering what was next. After some fasting and prayer, my wife and I decided to take a step of faith and start a discipleship ministry. We called it Deeper Walk Ministries. It focused on three main issues:

1. Helping Christians become more biblically literate
2. Teaching Christians how to live in the Spirit rather than the flesh
3. Training people to deal with the emotional and spiritual baggage that often kept them stuck

About a year into this journey, I received an invitation to become the president of a spiritual warfare counseling ministry called ICBC. It had been founded by Dr. Mark Bubeck, whose book *The Adversary* presented a biblically balanced approach to spiritual warfare. I had a lot of respect for him and what he had done to help people understand the role spiritual warfare plays in all of our lives. I accepted the position, and we combined the ministries to form what is today Deeper Walk International.

In this new position, I was privileged to meet many amazing mental health professionals, as well as biblical counselors and prayer ministers. One of the people I got to know was Dr. Jim Wilder. His research on the brain and his groundbreaking work in treating some of the most damaged people on the planet got me connected to neuroscience and attachment theory at a level I could never have foreseen.

WHY THIS BOOK?

For most of my adult life, I have been collecting tools to help people experience the breakthrough they long to experience. There is a temptation to offer people a one-size-fits-all experience that guarantees a breakthrough, but the reality is that people are often helped by a wide variety of strategies. Here are some examples of people who got significant help from many different approaches.

A military veteran with PTSD was struggling deeply with thoughts of suicide. He met with a prayer minister who helped him identify several root lies he was believing, and through listening prayer he was able to replace those lies with truth. He experienced a breakthrough that day and left the session smiling and feeling like himself for the first time in months. Helping him identify and replace the core beliefs driving his depression broke the cycle in which he had been trapped.

A friend of mine met with a woman who had a severe eating disorder for which she had been hospitalized. They met for a prayer session and ended up dealing with a demon that manifested as he pressed into some core issues in her life. He was able to lead her through prayers of renunciation and eviction that left her completely free. Getting rid of the wicked spirit ended her disorder instantly. In her case, a demon was at the root of her problems, and only a spiritual warfare strategy was going to work.[4]

A woman who was so depressed she qualified for federal disability assistance often struggled just to get out of bed in the morning. However, she was able to go to a residential treatment facility and started doing group work on a daily basis. The leader led the group to gradually increase the amount of time they could sit still and quiet their racing minds. The first day, all she could do was quiet her mind for five seconds at a time. Within a month, she was quieting for three to five minutes at a time. In addition to growing her ability to experience a quiet mind, the group began telling joy stories and practicing exercises to increase appreciation and joy. Within a few months, she was helping to lead these group sessions. Today, she teaches people the principles and practices of emotional and relational resilience.[5]

A pastor who once told a layman that taking an antidepressant was screaming to God, "I don't trust You," went through his own battle with anxiety and depression and later wrote, "I can honestly say that making the decision to take an antidepressant during [a dark] period in my life has been one of *the best* decisions I have ever made. It really has clarified my thinking, made me way less of an emotional basket case and allowed me to make better decisions. I'm not ashamed of the fact I am taking an antidepressant and have done a complete 180 in regards to how I used to feel about them."[6]

One of the patterns I have seen through the years is that people often experience a breakthrough because of a specific strategy and then turn that one strategy into the missing ingredient everyone needs in order to find freedom and healing. I have no problem with ministries having a focus on one strategy or another, but we all need a broader understanding of how these strategies work together and why one strategy may be more effective than another, depending on the root issue that needs to be addressed.

This book has been written to provide a model that applies not only to addiction recovery but to any area where someone feels stuck and needs to find a breakthrough. My prayer is that it will help both those looking for a breakthrough and those whose ministry is walking alongside Christians who feel stuck.

DEFINING BREAKTHROUGH: STRAIGHT LINE OR SPIRAL?

A breakthrough can happen at one of three levels. Each level focuses on a different core issue:

LEVEL 1: Relieve pain by focusing on symptoms
LEVEL 2: Repair damage by focusing on root issues
LEVEL 3: Rebuild maturity by focusing on new habits

Relieving pain is primarily about treating symptoms. Many people just want the pain to stop, which is completely legitimate. However, if we stop there, most of us will never experience the deeper levels of breakthrough we really need. Repairing damage is about getting at root issues such as trauma, lies we believe, and sins we have justified. Pain relief is often impossible without addressing such issues. Rebuilding maturity is about developing habits we lack. Long-lasting breakthrough is as much about the habits we build as the repair we experience.

According to my friend and clinical psychologist Dan Rumberger, most of us think of emotional healing as a straight line. We believe that every time we experience a breakthrough, we should move forward to a new level of victory and not look back. But this is seldom how things work. Far more often, our journey looks like a spiral in which we revisit memories and emotions again and again, but each time from a different perspective and with a different level of emotional capacity.[7]

It can feel like we are back to square one when we find ourselves falling into the same temptation or losing the same battle with a big emotion after we thought we had experienced a breakthrough. But just because we are facing a similar battle or experiencing a similar scenario does not mean we have made no progress. It can mean that we are revisiting an issue because there is another layer of work God wants to do.

TIME TO DIVE IN

I am excited to share the lessons I have learned and the journey I continue to be on. I don't think you ever arrive at a point where you say, "That's it. I've got it all figured out now." This book isn't meant to be a final answer but a contribution to the cause. If you are tracking with what you have read so far, I think you are going to enjoy the rest of the journey as we dive into big picture concepts and practical strategies that help people find the breakthrough they need.

Blessings,
Marcus Warner

CHAPTER 1

FINDING SOLUTIONS THAT WORK

A FEW YEARS AGO, the director of a recovery ministry at one of the largest churches in my area asked to meet for coffee. Because I have taught about spiritual warfare ministry for over thirty years, he specifically wanted to talk about the role of spiritual warfare in addiction. His specialty was helping men who were in bondage to pornography, but he found that about a year into this highly regarded program, a lot of men stalled. They often started the journey with a lot of hope and excitement, but many of them hit a wall partway into the process. He wondered if warfare might be the missing ingredient that would give them the breakthrough they needed.

I was impressed that he asked. It is easy to dismiss the role of demons in our modern world. There are also way too many people doing some pretty crazy things in the name of spiritual warfare. (I think of the man who said wearing aluminum foil on your head keeps demons from reading your mind.) So, it is understandable why some people would be skeptical and want nothing to do with the subject. I know too many Christians who have been wounded by the type of warfare ministry they have experienced.

I told this director that, in my experience, spiritual warfare often played a key role in addiction recovery. I have personally seen people experience significant breakthroughs by evicting demons and have heard numerous firsthand stories of others whose addictions ended when demons were removed. There is no question in my mind that spiritual warfare can play a very important role in the recovery process.

He agreed and invited me to talk to his group about the role of warfare in recovery. He then asked me a broader question. He was curious to know how I would design a recovery ministry. The timing of this conversation was interesting to me.

I had just met with leaders from two other large recovery ministries who were having similar problems. They saw people get off to a quick start and then hit a wall after several months. In each case, they ran programs that were high on accountability and mental renewal but were clearly missing other strategies (like spiritual warfare) that were just as important. His question got me thinking about the various tools I had collected through the years and the various principles I had learned. His question played a big role in getting me to write this book.

In the chapters ahead, I will explain a model that applies not only to addiction recovery but to any situation in which we are looking for a breakthrough from the issues that have us in bondage. For now, I want to focus on some of the challenges that keep our Christian solutions from being more effective in solving common problems people face.

THE LIMITS OF VULNERABILITY AND ACCOUNTABILITY

When recovery programs are heavy on vulnerability and accountability, they emphasize being honest about our struggles and having a team of people who hold us accountable for our behavior. This process often helps people get off to a good start, but without adding a few other important strategies, people tend to stall.

The Challenge with Vulnerability

One problem I have seen with an emphasis on vulnerability is that group time is often spent with everyone talking about the worst experiences and worst emotions they felt that week. At first, it can be liberating to discover that you are not alone in your battles. But when this is the only thing that happens week after week, it can begin to create second-hand trauma for both the leader and the other participants.

I once led a marriage retreat just for couples who led groups for the recovery ministry in their church. Out of curiosity, I asked how many of them thought they would likely quit within the year, and nearly every hand in the room went up. When I asked them what their group time was like, they all described a setting in which everyone shared their deepest struggles and biggest challenges week after week. It was creating a burden too great for them to bear, and they were all looking for an escape.

I asked if it was okay to take one of our sessions and model a different way to lead group time, and they enthusiastically agreed. I was able to walk them through a three-step model based on the pamphlet *Passing the Peace* that was created by Dr. Jim Wilder.[1]

First, I had them get into groups and take several minutes for each person to share one of their happiest memories involving time at a lake or a beach. Within a few minutes, the room was filled with laughter, and you could feel the positive energy filling the room.

Next, I had them close their eyes and ask Jesus if there was anything He wanted them to know about a struggle they were facing. I told them to write down the thoughts that came to their minds when they prayed. I also told them not to worry about whether it was obviously from God because that could be sorted out later.

Third, I had them share with the group what they had written—or at least what they felt comfortable sharing. In this way, instead of focusing simply on their struggles and the hard emotions they created, they were able to focus on God's perspective and His wisdom about their struggle. It also gave people the opportunity to either affirm or challenge what was shared as they were asked, "Does that sound like something God would want you to know?"

For example, someone might write, "I gave in to the temptation to look at porn, but five minutes into it, I said, 'What am I doing? This is not who I want to be. God, what do You want me to know about this?' The thought that came to my mind was that it was like me to want to resist temptation and that He was proud of me for stopping so quickly. He was also happy that I was sharing the experience with Him and not trying to hide it."

Another person might write, "I gave in to the temptation to look at porn this week, and when I asked God what He wanted me to know about that, the thoughts that came into my mind were, 'Of course, you did. You are a fraud. You pretend to be a good Christian, but this is what you really are.'" By sharing this, the people in the group are able to say, "That doesn't sound like God. That sounds like the enemy. Why don't you renounce that as a lie and ask God for the truth."

When the groups finished their conversations, I asked them for feedback. Most people said they felt a much greater sense of peace than they had before the exercise. Some said they felt like they had hope. No one reported feeling greater confusion or greater trauma. When I asked them if they would still quit if their group experiences were like this, they all said no. What they had just experienced was life-giving. It increased their joy and peace. What they had been doing before was draining, and they had all had enough.

The Challenge with Accountability

In addition to vulnerability, many recovery ministries stress accountability. I have met many people who raved about the impact their accountability team has had on their walk with God and their success in overcoming their addictions. I do not doubt them at all. But when I press into the issue a little deeper, what I hear them describe has almost nothing to do with accountability and everything to do with relational attachment.

The strategy that is actually giving them the strength to walk in victory is not accountability; it is the deep joy bonds they create with others on a similar journey. Many of these groups don't even ask accountability questions anymore. They just like getting together. The joy of their friendship fills a void in their lives that makes it easier for them to resist the temptations of pornography or alcohol or meth, or some other addiction. It is not the fear of failure that motivates them so much as the joy of connection. Their group forms an identity around the idea that we are a people who are there for each other no matter what happens.

Accountability is good for short-term task improvement. For example, I needed to be held accountable to practice the trumpet when I was in junior high. But I never progressed beyond that. Playing the trumpet never became a passion, and I never developed a bond with others who played instruments so that being a musician became part of my identity. Without those, accountability was only going to get me so far. In the same way, if we never progress beyond accountability to an identity that says we are part of a people who are honest with our failings but know that we are not defined by our failings, accountability alone will only get us so far. We need the transformational power that comes from belonging and a healthy group identity.

If the term *group identity* is new to you, I will discuss it more in the chapter on increasing joy bonds. My main point here is that attachment and the sense of identity that comes from who we see as "our people" is a major driver in the way we live.

FOUR GOOD IDEAS THAT NEUTRALIZED
WESTERN CHRISTIANITY

One of the reasons many of our models for recovery and emotional healing have holes in them is that Western Christianity itself has some holes that we often don't recognize. In our book *The Solution of Choice*, Jim Wilder and I make the case that the Enlightenment had an impact on the church that is still felt to this day.[2] It changed how we think about ourselves as Christians and what we see as core to the faith. In the process, it changed the solutions we offer to people with problems. To be specific, the Enlightenment and the philosophies that it spawned introduced four good ideas that, in many ways, have neutralized much of the impact of Western Christianity. The next few pages are going to get a little deep, but if you enjoy understanding how our culture got to where it is, I think you will find them worthwhile.

1. Reason

The Enlightenment taught us that the most important thing about being human was our ability to reason. We were different than animals—not because we were created in the image of God and designed for a relationship with Him—but because we could think. When the French Revolution abandoned the church, they made a statue of Sophia—the goddess of reason—and placed it in the cathedral of Notre Dame. They were making a statement: *From now on, we will worship reason rather than the Christian God.*

While the church did not worship reason in the same way the secular culture did, the church did make a shift in relation to reason. In response to the culture, we put far more emphasis on truth and rationality as the centerpiece of the faith. Instead of placing a deep attachment to God at the center, we placed reason at the center and asked correct thinking to produce a deep attachment to God. But life doesn't work like that. We don't think our way to attachment. Rather, attachment informs the way we think.

As a result of the new emphasis on reason, we sent our pastors to school, but not so they could learn how to build healthy communities or guide Christians to be the sort of people who love their neighbors well. We sent them to school to make sure they had a rational faith and good theology. We wanted to make sure our pastors were good at thinking because our theology was under attack on several fronts. There is nothing wrong with having good theology. In fact, it is vital to the faith. But biblical scholarship should not be valued more than love. Paul warned us that knowledge puffs up, but love builds up (1 Cor. 8:1).

So, what was the fruit of this shift toward reason? Did our focus on biblical truth and sound theology produce more mature Christians? Did it help the church become more Christlike? Or did it lead to more and more division? Did we make scholarship more important than discipleship? I ask this as a pastor with two master's degrees and a doctorate who taught college and seminary classes. I am not anti-academic. The question is: *Does reason belong at the center of the faith?*

A rational faith is clearly a good idea. Truth is important. But was it meant to be the hub of the wheel? Or did we move something to the center that was meant to be a spoke on the wheel?

2. Will

The second good idea that neutralized Western Christianity was the idea that the will is even more fundamental than reason to both our humanity and our faith. Many of the early Protestant movements sprang up in the days following the Enlightenment. Puritanism and revivalism were both anchored in a philosophy called *voluntarism* (from the Latin word for "will"). This philosophical movement believed that willpower or volition should be at the center of the Christian faith. The core textbook used in all of the Ivy League schools of the 1600s was *The Marrow of Christian Theology* by William Ames. He taught that the will was foundational to virtue and wrote, "Virtue is a habit whereby the will is inclined to do well."[3]

For the last four hundred years, Bible-believing Christians (like me) have tended to reduce many core concepts to acts of the will alone. But in most cases, there is something deeper going on than mere will.

The problem with reducing something like love or joy to mere choices is that there is so much more to them than the decisions we make. Today, we tend to encourage people to anchor their sense of eternal security in a choice they made at a point in time. But I can't think of a time that Paul told someone, "Remember the choice you made all those years ago and start making choices consistent with it." On the other hand, Paul often reminded people of the relational bond that had been formed with him (Phil. 1:8; 2 Cor. 12:15), with other believers (Eph. 4:3; Col. 2:2), and especially with Christ (1 Cor. 6:17; Rom. 6:5; Phil. 2:1). Based on these deep attachments, he encouraged Christians to live a life worthy of their calling (Eph. 4:1). It is not that choices have no role in this process, it is just not the deepest part of what is going on.

The other problem with putting too much focus on the will is that, for most of us, willpower and decision-making are pretty fickle allies. A person can swear he will never look at a naked woman online again and find himself doing it again the same day. I can tell myself I am going to do a better job of loving my wife, but if I am relying solely on willpower to do that, I'm likely to be frustrated. There are choices I can make that will make the attachment that love creates possible, but the attachment itself is deeper than a mere choice.

Most pastors know that teaching the Bible and calling people to make good decisions is often futile. Sometimes it falls on deaf ears, and sometimes people make choices in the moment but don't follow through on them for more than a few weeks at best.

I have attended many services at which hundreds and even thousands of people have gone forward to make a commitment to change the way they live, only to fail to follow through on that choice in the following months. I myself have gone forward in response to a sermon and made a choice to make some kind of life change, only to fall back into old patterns of behavior relatively quickly.

When we don't see much change from truth and an appeal to the will, we generally turn to accountability. One church leader heard I was working on a discipleship curriculum and encouraged me to "put some teeth in it." Specifically, he meant I should be sure to make accountability a core feature of the curriculum. It is an understandable suggestion, but as I wrote earlier in this chapter, accountability is not as effective at producing life change as most of us think. To this day, evangelicals tend to see life through the lens of voluntarism, which sees beliefs as the root of all our emotions and choices as the key to life change. While both truth and wise decisions are good ideas, there is something deeper than both of them: our bond, union, or attachment with God. The true hub of the faith is our union with Christ, which makes us one with God.

3. Power

The third good idea that neutralized Western Christianity was the idea that power is the missing ingredient that keeps us from real transformation. While reason and will have dominated evangelical churches, a focus on Holy Spirit power has tended to dominate charismatic churches. Many have embraced the idea that reason and power don't work because we lack Holy Spirit power. But there is more to the Holy Spirit than power, and power does not produce maturity.

Following the Enlightenment and the trend toward voluntarism, the next philosophical movement we saw in the secular world was modernism. One of the prophets of this movement was Friedrich Nietzsche. As a young man, he was deeply influenced by Arthur Schopenhauer's treatise, "The World as Will and Representation." Schopenhauer's book viewed the will as deeply irrational and more like a craving or a passion—like the sex drive or the lust for cruelty. He believed if these were not tamed, they would drive a person to misery.[4] Nietzsche came to despise Christianity's focus on love as weak and championed the idea of an *ubermensch* or superman who was able to assert his will through power. Thus, the power to make things happen became more valued than good ideas or well-intended decisions.

Ideas like those espoused by Nietzsche influenced the modern world. It is a common axiom in politics that you can't do the good you want to do until you win. So, accumulating power and cutting the moral corners you need to cut in order to win are justified as necessary "power moves" to accomplish a greater good. Power came to take a greater place of honor than either reason or the will in the modern age with devastating impact. More people died in the twentieth century than in the rest of human history combined because of the power moves of "utopian" visionaries like Hitler, Stalin, and Mao.

The new focus on power in culture was reflected in the church as well. We came to believe the reason that truth and choices didn't produce more fruit was that we lacked the Holy Spirit's power to make those decisions. But is that what the Bible teaches? Does it say the Holy Spirit will give us the power to be more obedient? Or does the Bible teach that a relationship with the Spirit—an attachment with God—naturally leads to a more obedient life? Walking in the Spirit is primarily a relational idea. Again, there is a place for power in the Christian life, but we have often asked it to do something it was not intended to do, and that is to produce maturity.

One needs only think through the long list of charismatic leaders who operated in tremendous power but did not demonstrate great maturity in their personal lives to see that power is not the key to maturity and transformation. Don't most of us know of someone who had amazing fruit in their ministry life but was a mess in their private life? Power produced a following and even led people to Christ, but that same power was not the key to personal transformation. Maturity is about relational and emotional intelligence that only comes with practice.

4. Tolerance

The postmodern generation that dominates culture today has largely given up on the idea that the church has any solutions for producing life change. Our kids have watched our lack of love, joy, peace, and self-control and come to the conclusion that Christianity doesn't really work. As a result, they have waved the white flag of surrender and said, "We should not expect people to change. Let's just tolerate everyone the way they are and not ask anyone to change."

Now, just as there is nothing wrong with a reasonable faith, or making good choices, or experiencing the Holy Spirit's power, there is nothing wrong with tolerance (unless it is redefined beyond recognition). I would define *tolerance* as doing good to people even if you disagree with them. Without disagreement there is nothing to tolerate. Unfortunately, more and more people define tolerance as agreeing with someone else's opinion simply because they have that opinion.

My point in taking this dive into culture has been to show that none of these four good ideas were meant to be at the center of the faith. That spot has always been reserved for a joyful love bond with God. The stronger and more joy-based that attachment is, the more fruit gets produced. When attachment is at the hub of the wheel, the spokes find their proper place and the wheel spins smoothly. But if Christianity is unable to produce life change in people, then something is missing from our model. If our Christianity is not making us more loving and patient people, who even form attachments with our enemies, then something about our faith is broken.

As I began to grasp more fully the impact of the Enlightenment and especially voluntarism on most of us Bible-believing Christians, I understood more clearly how it has warped many of the solutions we look to for personal breakthrough and offer to those in need. The model in this book is partly an attempt to correct the philosophical foundation that has driven much of what we do in trying to help ourselves and others find the breakthroughs we need and expand the type of solutions we offer.

For example, if an addict comes to one church, he may get a lot of good biblical advice and perhaps some accountability, but is that all he needs? Or, an addict may go to a "power" church and have a dramatic experience at the altar or in a counseling room, but again, is that all that is needed? If a person goes to a church that tells them change is impossible, they are certainly not going to get any help. The issue here is that too many Christians have come to the church looking for solutions to their problems only to leave with inadequate answers that leave a lot of them wondering if Christianity really works.

A MATURITY MODEL

A growth model works like a factory. It is designed to produce a specific product. Any successful factory will need to identify precisely the intended outcome and engineer strategies that predictably achieve that outcome. Our factory is designed to produce maturity and it follows five specific strategies.

Biblically speaking, *maturity* means *complete*. For example, Paul states that his desire in ministry is to "present everyone mature in Christ" (Col. 1:28 ESV). The word *mature* in this verse is *teleios*. At its root, it is related to the idea of reaching a desired goal.[5] Thus, when a child becomes an adult, they are said to be *teleios* (1 Cor. 14:20).[6] In a similar way, a plant is mature when it is in bloom, and fruit is mature when it is ripe. They have reached their intended destination and are thus complete.

Emotional maturity is primarily about two areas of development. First, it is about developing a strong identity. Second, it is about developing the skills and capacity needed to regulate our emotions.

> **Strong Identity** (both my identity in Christ and my group identity as a kingdom citizen)
>
> **+**
>
> **Skills** (relational skills and emotional regulation skills)
> _____
>
> **Maturity** (the capacity to act like myself and regulate my emotions)

Identity

Emotional maturity can be defined as the ability to act like myself, even under stress. To understand this, it can help to look at the process by which our sense of identity grows from birth to adulthood.

As babies, the part of our brains that knows who we are is largely undeveloped. This part of the brain grows through thousands of relational experiences. The driving force behind our identity development is attachment. As babies bond to their mothers and fathers, sisters and brothers, grandparents, and aunts and uncles, these attachments form a collection of memories that tell the baby: *This is who you are. These are your people. You are like them.* For example, growing up in the Warner family, we had lots of deep conversations. My dad was a professor who became a college president. My mom was also an educator. But we were also good at making each other laugh. It was like us to sit around the table and see who could tell the most entertaining story or make the family laugh. It was an especially big win if we got Dad to laugh. We knew if we got him laughing, he would start telling us all of his "dad jokes," which we all know by heart to this day.

One of the primary developmental processes that is absolutely crucial when we are infants and toddlers is the formation of an organized sense of self—or a core identity. When little ones do not develop a strong sense of self, they will learn to adopt a totally different *persona* depending on the emotion they feel. In a sense, the baby turns into a different person with every upsetting emotion they experience. Instead of learning to live with an integrated, organized core identity that allows them to act like themselves regardless of how they feel, they develop an unstable identity that changes with every mood they feel.

For example, one of a toddler's personas can be angry and easily throw temper tantrums. This was me. Before I was ten years old, I was notorious in the Warner family for my tantrums. I remember my parents wondering what in the world to do with me. I could be a compliant, happy, relationally engaged child one minute, then snap and throw myself on the floor screaming the next.

The primary solution to tantrums (especially in the toddler years) is not disciplining the child. (See *The 4 Habits of Raising Joy-Filled Kids* for more on this.[7]) The primary solution is meeting them in their angry, out-of-control state and helping them regulate their emotions. If our toddlers don't get help with this, their brains will never learn the skill of recovering from anger, and they will continue to handle their anger with the emotional maturity of a small child for the rest of their lives or until that skill set is learned. In my case, I remember my older sister teaching me how to count to ten and take a deep breath, and actually practicing with me so I could learn to control my anger.

Toddlers and young children need to be helped to learn how to regulate all of their emotions. This means they need to be taught skills, but it also means someone needs to stay relationally engaged with them when they get overwhelmed. In their book *How We Love*, Milan and Kay

Yerkovic make the sad observation that among the hundreds of couples they have led through marital counseling, very few of them had even a single memory of someone staying relationally engaged with them as they recovered from any upsetting emotion during their childhood years. They learned to ask each of their clients a simple question, "Can you recall being comforted as a child after a time of emotional distress?"[8] It was surprising how few had even one memory of such an experience. This means that most of the people they worked with did not get good training on how to regulate their emotions. As a result, they were still stuck in child- or infant-level maturity.

Without the proper maturity development, people will lack the skills and capacity to deal with their emotions. This kind of immaturity makes it almost impossible to act like ourselves when things go wrong. It also makes it much more likely that we will get stuck in unwanted emotions with no idea how to recover.

Our Identity in Christ

It is worth noting that if someone has a grossly underdeveloped sense of identity because of neglect or abuse in their early years, simply teaching them facts about their identity in Christ is not going to have the same impact as it will for someone who has a more stable identity already formed. The brain's sense of identity is not formed by information but rather by attachment. What we believe about ourselves is important, but when it comes to identity formation there is something even deeper than our beliefs. When we learn to form joy-filled attachments *and* we get our beliefs anchored in our identity in Christ, we have a powerful one-two punch that makes for a very stable sense of self.

Later in this book, I will unpack more of the brain science related to attachment and identity. For now, it may help to think of the left brain as where our narratives about life are stored (i.e., our beliefs) and the right brain as where attachments are formed and our sense of group identity develops. Bringing the two parts of the brain together for a healthy core identity might look like this:

LEFT BRAIN NARRATIVE	RIGHT BRAIN ATTACHMENT
I am deeply loved by God.	I feel safe and secure.
I am a child of God.	I feel peace.
It is like me to love others well.	I can bounce back from hard emotions.
My people return good for evil.	I share joy with others easily.

Regulation

The second developmental task that is essential to maturity development is *emotional regulation*. The more mature we are, the more it takes for us to blow up, shut down, or melt down. Thus, part of maturity development is learning to know who we are or developing a healthy identity. The other part is emotional regulation, in which we develop the skills and capacity to remain who we are under stress.

The two work together like this:

IDENTITY

Develop a healthy
identity.

RESILIENCE

Let that identity drive the
way I handle emotions.

Most of our emotional regulation skills are learned in infancy and childhood. As babies, we cannot regulate our emotions at all. We are completely dependent on someone else to recognize what is wrong and do whatever is necessary to help us recover. This is why parents spend so much time learning to recognize the slightest nuances in their baby's behavior. We notice when they are fussy or perplexed or angry or overwhelmed. We learn to read their body language so that we can identify what they need and take care of that need. Babies who get well cared for emotionally and physically without having to ask learn that safe, secure attachments are normal. It lays a foundation for emotional stability throughout life. If a baby does not get these needs met, it will promote emotional instability, and the damage will need to be repaired later in life.

As babies become toddlers, their emotions get more intense. Anger can become rage. Fear can become terror. Sadness can become a sobbing mess. If our reaction to this is simply to try to shut it down and tell them, "No!" or say things like, "Big boys don't cry," we will stunt their maturity development because they will never learn how to properly recover from such emotions. The better response is to meet them in their big emotion, stay relationally engaged with them, and comfort them until they start acting like themselves again. As we do this for them, their brains watch what is going on and learn to imitate it. If we simply get angry at them or shame them for their emotions, they will learn to get angry at themselves or shame themselves for feeling those emotions. Such reactions can become lifelong habits.

As children age, we don't take care of all of their emotional needs as if they were still infants. We begin to train them how to take care of themselves and regulate their own emotions. We teach them how to use their words to accurately name what they are feeling. We teach them how to take deep breaths and count to ten and help them practice all sorts of skills that will enable them to manage their emotions with skill.

HOLES IN OUR MATURITY

If a child gets all of this training, maturity happens almost automatically. It is a natural result of watching mature people, learning skills from those people, and practicing them over and over again with help. However, missing any of this and going through unresolved pain will stunt the maturity process and leave us with holes in our maturity. As a result, most people who are looking for a breakthrough in their lives may not realize it, but they need more than relief. They need to build their maturity and fill the holes created by trauma.

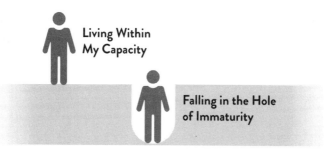

Living Within
My Capacity

Falling in the Hole
of Immaturity

Most of us have holes in our maturity. We missed something (or a lot of things) when we were kids. As a result, we can find ourselves walking along, feeling fine, and acting like ourselves, then suddenly, we get triggered, fall into a hole, and find ourselves acting like a child instead of an adult. We didn't consciously choose to do this. It just sort of happened. Learning to recognize when we fall into these holes can help us determine where our growth edge is. If I find that I fall into a hole when I get sad, but not so much when I feel disgust, it lets me know that I need to work on my ability to deal with sadness. That should become my focus. This means I should start watching how people who recover well from sadness do it. I should get some skill training from a coach. I will likely also need to meet with a prayer minister to uncover any roots that make this particular emotion so difficult.

In some ways, this whole book is meant to answer the question: *How does a person fill the holes in their maturity development?* The models and strategies presented here all play a role in that process.

In the next chapter we will take a closer look at some common growth models used by Christians to provide solutions for the problems we face. Growth models are important, not only because they suggest solutions for our problems, but because they limit the solutions we believe are possible. One of my core goals in writing this book is to help us understand the bigger picture of what people need in order to experience lasting breakthrough and why a variety of strategies are often necessary. In order to better understand the growth model proposed in this book, it will help to see how it compares and contrasts with other common growth models.

CHAPTER 2

GROWTH MODELS

A GROWTH MODEL is a comprehensive approach to transformation. Every growth model is built on a philosophy that is anchored in a specific worldview. In Christian circles, nearly all of them will call their worldview "biblical," which can be confusing because they are often very different from each other. It is not uncommon for Bible-believing Christians to embrace widely different growth models.

In their book *How People Grow*, Henry Cloud and John Townsend identify four growth models that have been commonly embraced in the evangelical church. These are the sin model, the truth model, the experiential model, and the supernatural model.[1] Let's take a look at these so we can see how they compare to the model I will teach in the rest of the book.

THE SIN MODEL

From a biblical perspective, all of our problems started when sin entered the world. Thus, sin is the original problem from which all other problems arise. Therefore, it seems pretty obvious that dealing with sin is the primary task of biblical counseling.

There is a lot of truth in this. Most of our problems are either caused by our own sin or by the effects of the sins of others. At a basic level, repentance is how we deal with our own sin and forgiveness is how we deal with the sins of others—especially those sins that wound us deeply. Cloud and Townsend sum up the sin model in three statements:

1. God is good.
2. You're bad.
3. Stop it.[2]

This model has often been the source of a lot of humor. If you have ever seen Bob Newhart play the role of psychologist Robert Hartley in the 1970s, you may have also watched a scene Newhart did decades later for a comedy sketch series. In it, he reprises his role and meets with a client who has a fear of being trapped in a box or buried alive. She says, "I just start thinking about being buried alive, and I begin to panic." He quickly offers her a diagnosis and says, "You're claustrophobic," then tells her he is going to say two words that will change her life. He tells her to listen very carefully, then says, "Stop it!"[3] That's it. It's the only advice he has.

While oversimplifications like this are easy to mock, there is a lot of truth in the sin model. Whether it is dealing with our own sin or with sins committed against us, a lot of what we have to process in counseling is related to sin.

For example, if we are creating problems for ourselves because we cannot control our sinful behavior, there is nothing wrong with engaging in some behavior modification strategies. My friend Juni Felix, author of *You Are Worth the Work*, teaches the science of behavior design and often shares a method called "Tiny Habits." The idea is that most of us are trying to build habits to change behavioral patterns in our lives, but we focus on big changes like, "I'm going to lose weight." That is a worthy goal, but Juni would argue that it is too abstract and needs to be broken down into much smaller and simpler objectives.[4]

We might decide that in order to lose weight, we are going to stop eating sugar. But that is still a pretty big step. Strategy one might be to order one scoop of ice cream instead of two and then celebrate that healthy self-care decision by taking a deep breath and saying, "Well done!" A second strategy might be keeping "happy replacement snacks" with us to satisfy cravings. It is also important to take some time to intentionally celebrate every time we succeed at moving toward your healthy aspiration. Once we master a Tiny Habit, we can design another habit "recipe" to complement the first. It's just like planting a seed in the right soil and intentionally caring for it each day. As we incrementally build this "success momentum" and realize we can create healthy habits, it won't take long before we will begin to see real transformation in our weight loss and health and wellness goals. It is the same with other issues, where change is needed. Good behavior modification strategies can be really helpful.

The challenge with the sin model is that we can ask too much from it. We can reduce all of our problems to dealing with sin. This may mean becoming so focused on behavior that we miss what is going on below the surface. It might mean becoming legalistic and blaming things on sin that are not actually anchored in sin. Just as the Pharisees assumed sin was the cause of a man's blindness (see John 9), we can find ourselves shaming people and loading them with false guilt by assuming any emotional struggle they have is a sin issue.

For example, when I was in a season of battling anxiety and looking for relief, someone told me, "You know fear is a sin. We are commanded not to be afraid over 150 times in the Bible."[5] On the one hand, this person was right. The Bible does say something like, "Do not be afraid" over 150 times, and grammatically these are generally written in the imperative form, which is the form of a command. However, this does not mean that fear is always a sin. These statements were written primarily as challenges and encouragement. Joshua was being encouraged to be strong and courageous in the face of scary situations (Deut 31:23; Josh 1:6, 9). He was not being told he would be in sin or punished if he felt fear. When our children get scared by storms and we say, "Don't be afraid," we are not giving them commands. We are not going to punish them if they feel fear. We are trying to comfort them. Turning fear into a sin didn't do anything to resolve my fear. It just added a layer of guilt and shame on top of the fear.

While there is clearly truth in the sin model, there is more to emotional healing and maturity development than dealing with sin. This model addresses some important issues, but can become damaging if we never progress beyond sin management.

THE TRUTH MODEL

This approach to transformation is anchored in Christ's amazing promise that "the truth will set you free" (John 8:32). Many people have taken this verse to mean that truth is the only thing that will set you free, and they reduce all change models to truth models. Cloud and Townsend write, "Passages that emphasize knowing truth, renewing your mind, and how you 'think in your heart' became a new theology of 'thinking truth to gain emotional health.'"[6]

For years, I taught the truth model. I embraced the idea that beliefs were the foundation of all of our emotions and behavior:

- If we had a problem in our relationship with God, the solution was to change our view of God.
- If we struggled with self-worth, the solution was to change our view of ourselves.
- If we got angry easily, we needed to change the beliefs that blamed others for blocking our goals.
- If we were depressed, we needed to change the beliefs that told us joy was impossible.

Sometimes, changing our beliefs is exactly the right solution to our problems. But as we will see in the next chapter, there are other engines involved in driving our emotions. Not everything is quite as simple as changing what we believe to be true. This having been said, there is a lot to be gained by learning to see life through the lens of a biblical worldview.

DISCIPLESHIP AND CULTURE

Our approach to discipleship will always be anchored in our growth model. If we embrace a sin model, that will inform our approach to discipleship. If we embrace a truth model, that will drive our approach to the process. It helps me to think of discipleship as a form of cultural assimilation. It works like this.

1. Conversion

When we become Christians, we leave one culture (the kingdom of darkness) and take up citizenship in another culture (the kingdom of God). Thus, Paul can say we have been rescued from the dominion of darkness and brought into the kingdom of God's beloved Son (Col. 1:13) or that we have died to life as slaves of sin and been reborn to life as God's children (Rom. 6; Gal. 4).

Just as someone who is raised in one culture and moves to a foreign culture has to adapt to the behaviors, values, and beliefs of their new environment, so Christians have to adapt to becoming strangers and foreigners in this world (1 Peter 1:17). If someone moves to a new culture and does not adapt, then they don't really assimilate. They just keep on living with their old customs and ideas. Discipleship is about assimilating into the kingdom. It requires dying to our life as citizens of the world in order to think and act as citizens of the kingdom. Sadly, the church is filled with people who have changed citizenship without assimilating into kingdom culture. They still live like this world is their home.

2. Belonging

In becoming citizens of the kingdom, we become part of a new group that gives us a new identity. Our people change. We are no longer of the world. Our people are now all of the other people who have been born into the family of God. Belonging to God's people becomes the foundation for changing our beliefs, values, and behaviors.

3. Worldview

One of the reasons Jesus became flesh was to bring us light. In other words, we were blind and living in darkness. We were looking at life through the wrong set of lenses and needed a new perspective. He came to correct our view of how life worked. He wanted us to learn the worldview of the kingdom of God. Thus, an essential part of discipleship is learning to think like citizens of the kingdom of heaven.

4. Values

What we believe to be important, good, and beautiful are rooted in our worldview. A kingdom worldview teaches us what God sees as good and excellent. The Bible routinely contrasts the wise who agree with God's values and fools who rebel against God's worldview to embrace their own values. The prodigal son is the classic story of a young man who rejected the worldview and values of his father because he was fully convinced he knew better than his father where to find the good life. He is the archetypal fool. However, through humility and repentance, he renewed his relationship with his father, was reinitiated into the family, and began to embrace the values that flowed from his identity as a son. Thus, he became wise. In the same way, discipleship is the process of learning to embrace the worldview and values of the kingdom so that we may become wise.

5. Behavior

The outward sign of the inward transformation that is produced by conversion, belonging, worldview, and values are the habits we form and the lifestyle we develop. In many parts of the church, we have gotten this discipleship model backward. We start with behavioral expectations, then go to values, then to worldview, and we end with belonging. It creates a legalistic approach to Christianity in which belonging must be earned and, in some cases, salvation itself must be maintained through good behavior.

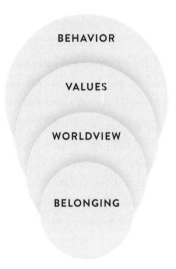

It is worth taking a moment here to highlight the connection between belonging and beliefs. Belonging is a powerful factor in forming our beliefs. Whatever group I see myself as belonging to will shape what I believe. If I see my people in terms of politics, I will be inclined to believe what my people believe and value what my people value. I will also tend to treat those outside of my group as "the enemy." This is precisely what Jesus was warning against in the Sermon on the Mount when He said it is easy to love our own people (Matt 5:44–48). The challenge lies in loving those who are *not* our people.

The purpose of discipleship is to build such a strong attachment to Jesus and His people that our connection to His kingdom supersedes all other attachments. Discipleship should help us build a strong sense of belonging that shapes our identity in a way that overrides any political, ethnic, or social identities. Thus, the worldview and values of the kingdom must mold how we approach everything else. Far too often, the influence moves in the other direction. The political, ethnic, and social groups to which we belong mold what we believe Christianity should be. Because we all have a tendency to assume that our group has it right, it can be a very tricky process to navigate.

My guess is that you know someone who completely flipped theologically when they went to college and became part of a different culture. This doesn't happen simply because of what they are taught in the classroom but because of the social pressure to conform and the joy that is found in belonging. There is a price to pay for going against the flow of any culture (or subculture). There are also social and emotional rewards for going along with the group. This is why Jesus called His disciples to count the cost of following Him and warned us that following Him may even cost us family relationships (Matt 10:34–39; 16:24–27). He Himself was crucified for refusing to bow to the social pressure of His day. He warned His disciples on the eve of His crucifixion not to be surprised when they were hated and persecuted because they were following a master who was hated and persecuted (John 15:18–20).

One of the reasons for taking the time to look at the relationship between belonging and beliefs is to demonstrate that as important as beliefs are to the way we feel, those beliefs are often driven by the social pressure of the group we are in. This is one of the reasons Paul warned us not to be misled: "Bad company corrupts good character" (1 Cor. 15:33). The book of Psalms starts with a similar warning to be careful which group we join. Walking with sinners, standing with the wicked, and sitting with mockers will shape us into people we do not want to be (Ps. 1:1–2).

THE EXPERIENTIAL MODEL

Cloud and Townsend use the label "experiential model" to describe inner healing prayer models. They write, "Proponents of the more spiritual versions of this model either took the pain [of their past] to Jesus or took Jesus to the pain. In a kind of emotional archaeology, people would dig up hurts from the past and then seek healing through prayer or imagery or just clearing out the pain."[7]

I know what they mean. Much of my ministry life has been spent helping people experience the presence of Jesus in a way that has brought healing to past traumas. The term "emotional archaeology" sounds a bit dismissive, though I can appreciate why Cloud and Townsend use it. Some ministries focus on finding painful memories, stirring them up, and then seeing if they can help people find Jesus. There has been a lot of fruit from these ministries and, at times, I have personally followed that formula and seen amazing results. But there is also a danger that we can stir up pain and not find Jesus or find the wrong Jesus. (I'll explain this more in a moment.) There is also a danger that we can reduce all emotional healing to finding the right memory and resolving the issues it created. Let's take a closer look at some problems that can arise in the experiential model.

Problem #1: We Can Stir Up the Pain Without Finding Jesus

There can be a tendency to want to help people find a breakthrough by going to the most painful memories they have or the earliest memories they have and trying to help them have an experience with Jesus to heal those memories. Sometimes this works, and the idea sounds reasonable. But the reality is that many people are not ready for that kind of process. It is dangerous to stir up the pain of core memories before people are ready to go there.

Instead of this approach, I recommend simply helping people establish a connection with Jesus and see where He wants to take them. For example, one woman who had some profound trauma in her past asked to meet with me. It was tempting to listen to her story and immediately ask her to pray about the root memory that was clearly fueling her pain. Instead, I invited her to ask Jesus to take her to any memory He chose. She closed her eyes and saw herself on an old swing set that she loved as a child. It was a happy place for her and brought up a flood of positive emotions. She then asked Jesus if there was anywhere else they needed to go. She sensed He wanted them to leave the swing set and go to the house. Room by room, He took her to various memories that had caused her pain and did something to heal what had happened. By the time He brought her to the place of her greatest trauma, she felt a deeper attachment and greater trust in Jesus than when she had started. By letting God's Spirit lead the process, we went in exactly the order God knew we needed to go instead of the order I might have expected.

I know of other people who took years to form a healthy attachment with Jesus before tackling any of their hard memories. In the end, the goal is not a process or a particular experience but a deeper trust and connection with Jesus.

Problem #2: We Can Lead People to the Wrong Jesus

I may be diving into the deep end here, but I think it is important to warn people that demons can masquerade as angels of light (2 Cor. 11:14). They can even pretend to be Jesus. There are many New Age practitioners who are more than happy to lead people to Jesus for healing. The problem is they are leading people to a counterfeit Jesus who is able to give them some kind of experience that will convince them they are with the Jesus of the Bible. However, such an encounter will eventually lead that person into bondage. The New Age Jesus will eventually (and sometimes immediately) lead the person to false doctrine—often universalism—and into a syncretistic approach to Christianity that uses Christian terms but fills them with pagan or mystical meanings.

Just because something is happening in a church or a Christian ministry and people are using the name of Jesus doesn't mean that every spiritual experience that happens there is legitimate. I know people who have encountered spirits presenting as saints, Mary, Jesus, deceased relatives, and angels, only to discover later that they had interacted with demons masquerading with deceptive identities.

One solution to this problem is to never practice listening prayer or any kind of spiritual experience. But I think a better approach than throwing the baby out with the bathwater is learning how to test spirits. One simple way to do this is to be direct and pray what I call an "if" prayer that goes something like this: "If this is the true Jesus who came in the flesh, died, and rose again, I thank You for doing what only You can do. But if this is a counterfeit and you are a spirit masquerading as Jesus, I command you to leave in the name of the true Jesus." I have seen this simple test expose many counterfeits. For example, one person seemed to encounter Jesus in her memory, but he just wasn't very helpful. In fact, he met her in the memory, touched her on the head, and made her fall asleep. This seemed odd because it felt like he was just avoiding the problem. When she prayed the "if" prayer, the false Jesus disappeared. She then invited the true Jesus to come, and He turned out to be very helpful.

I think God allows counterfeits in order to expose lies we have believed about Jesus. For example, I noticed a pattern in which the first "Jesus" to show up was often a caricature based on misconceptions about Him. One person who was raised in a legalistic home invited Jesus to help and said he looked angry and disgusted with him. Another person raised with prosperity gospel doctrine saw a floating Jesus with a golden sash hovering in the air. One even saw a strange Jesus who almost looked like a bug. When I asked him about it, he said he grew up in a home that didn't believe in religion. His family thought of Christianity as weird. It made sense that a weird Jesus showed up. All of them were seeing counterfeits based on false beliefs about Jesus.

Oddly enough, there is some advantage to people meeting a false Jesus before they meet the real one. Just like pearls are best displayed against a black background, the goodness of Jesus is often seen more clearly in contrast with the distortions. It helps people realize more clearly just how wrong their view of Christ has been and how amazing the real Jesus is.

Problem #3: We Can Reduce All Emotional Healing to Dealing with Root Memories

One of the dangers of any effective strategy is that we ask it to do too much. I remember meeting with a young man who had lost his parents as a teenager. He remembered sitting by himself after the funeral and feeling completely alone in the world. We did a listening prayer exercise, and when he closed his eyes and revisited the memory, he felt like Jesus was sitting next to him. I could see his breathing get deeper and his body relax. The God of all comfort had met him in his grief and brought him an unexpected level of peace.

The next time we met, I assumed we would do some more listening prayer together, but nothing seemed to happen. At that point, I had the thought, *You have more tools in your toolbox than just listening prayer.* We spent the session helping him understand his identity in Christ, and he said it was just what he needed.

Listening prayer as a tool for dealing with root memories is a key strategy for helping to repair the damage of past trauma. However, it is still not the only strategy needed for maturity development. The problem is not so much with the model itself as with people who want to make it the only model needed for breakthrough.

Problem #4: Even Miraculous Healing Events Don't Produce Instant Maturity in People

If a person is trapped in infant-level maturity before they have a supernatural experience with God, they will still be an emotional infant afterward. A breakthrough experience with God does not grant instant maturity. It removes the barrier that keeps them stuck and opens the door to move forward and grow. In many long healing journeys, there will be hundreds of "breakthrough" moments that all play a small role in making maturity possible. These longer journeys taught me that breakthrough is not an event for most people. It is not a moment or an experience that suddenly changes everything. Important breakthroughs all along the way play a role in the greater breakthrough that only comes over time as emotional capacity and secure attachments are developed.

THE SUPERNATURAL MODEL

The supernatural approach to breakthrough relies completely on two spiritual realities—the Holy Spirit and wicked spirits—to produce transformation. Cloud and Townsend write:

> Charismatics sought instant healing and deliverance; others depended on the Holy Spirit to make the change happen as he lived his life through them. Exchanged-life people (those who hold that you just get out of the way so Christ can reproduce his life in you) as well as other very well-grounded students of the spiritual life trusted God to lead them and make changes in them.[8]

Like the other models, this one exists because it often works—and because the Bible teaches the importance of walking in the Spirit and resisting the devil. In fact, there is no question that learning to live in the Spirit is an absolute essential in the transformation process. You may know people who had a supernatural experience and suddenly all of their cravings for drugs and alcohol disappeared. I know people whose eating disorders ended in a single deliverance session. In fact, one warfare practitioner I knew said he had helped so many people find freedom from their addictions he had almost single-handedly shut down a local counseling center. I have learned to take such claims with a grain of salt—but still, something profound was happening for such a claim to even have the appearance of credibility.

As with the other models, the problems come when you get out of balance or ask a model to do too much. We can come to believe that deliverance is the only tool people need in order to solve their problems or that if they simply learn how to live a crucified life in the power of the Spirit, everything else will fall into place. Clearly, these are good things, but they may not be the only things.

There are other growth models we could mention beyond the four introduced by Cloud and Townsend, but the point is that growth models matter. The purpose of this book is to introduce a growth model with a track record of helping people experience breakthroughs and transformation.

THE MATURITY MODEL

Christian maturity is relational. It is revealed in intimacy with God and in love for one another. In fact, the greatest demonstration of maturity possible is to love your enemies.

The Bible is actually pretty clear about this. Maturity is directly related to love. Jesus summed up the Law and the Prophets in two commands: love God and love your neighbor (Matt. 22:37–39; Mark 12:29–31). The centrality of these two commands can be seen with a quick look at the Ten Commandments. The first four commandments relate to loving God: (1) we are to have no other gods, (2) we are to make no graven images, (3) we are not to take His name in vain, and (4) we are to remember the Sabbath day to keep it holy (Ex. 20:1–11). The next six commands relate to loving your neighbor: (5) we are to honor our father and mother, and we are not to (6) murder, (7) steal, (8) commit adultery, (9) lie, or (10) covet (Ex. 20:12–17). The Ten Commandments themselves are a summary of the entire Torah, so in a very tangible way, the whole law is anchored in love.

The apostle Paul also identified love as "the most excellent way" (1 Cor. 12:31) and "the greatest of these" (1 Cor. 13:13). As Jesus taught us in the Golden Rule, love is about treating others the way you would want to be treated (Matt. 7:12). Earlier in the Sermon on the Mount, Jesus said it is easy to love those we think of as our "own people" (Matt. 5:46–47). But maturity is demonstrated by extending love to those who are not our own people. For His original audience the lines between "us" and "them" were pretty clear. Pharisees did not engage with "tax collectors and sinners" (Matt. 9:10–11). Jews did not interact with Samaritans (John 4:9). And none of them liked Romans. People often refused even to greet those who were not one of their own (Matt. 5:47). It was the norm to love your own people and hate your enemies (Matt. 5:43).

In stark contrast to this, Jesus told His followers to be *teleios*, or mature, just as His Father in heaven was *teleios* (Matt. 5:48). The standard for love—for maturity—was our heavenly Father who was good to those who loved Him and to those who hated Him. Thus, Jesus taught the radical idea that we should do good to everyone—to our own people, to those who are not our people, and even to those who hate us. Thus, we bless those who persecute us, pray for those who curse us, and love our enemies (Matt. 5:44–48; Luke 6:28, 35).

The glorification of romance has taught us to think of love as an emotion; it is the way you make me feel. Most evangelicals have been taught to think of love as the sacrificial choice to do the right thing. However, love cannot be reduced to either an emotion or a choice. It is more than that. Love is more accurately described as an attachment. Love means that I am bonded to you in a way that motivates me to treat you the way I would want to be treated, even if you don't see me the same way or treat me the same way. In this sense, maturity is measured by my ability to love you, even if you cause me to suffer. Thus, Jesus could say there is no greater love than to lay down your life for a friend (John 15:13).

Growth models are important because they determine which solutions we believe are essential to transformation. If our growth model is skewed, we may only deal with sin, lies, deliverance, or inner healing and miss obvious problems that need attention or offer solutions that don't really address the root issues involved. This is why we need to be careful not to reduce everything to a single root cause with a simple solution.

In the next chapter, we get to the heart of the book. I will put the whole maturity model together by looking at five engines that drive our emotions and point us to five different strategies for emotional healing. We will start with a look at two "composite characters" named Titus and Lisa who looked for help from traditional Christian growth models but who needed to learn how to build maturity.

CHAPTER 3

THE FIVE ENGINES THAT DRIVE OUR EMOTIONS

TITUS WAS NEWLY DIVORCED and searching for answers. His wife left him because he was never able to get control of his porn habit or his drinking. After eight years of feeling like she was all alone in their marriage, she had enough. She took the kids and moved in with her parents.

Titus had grown up going to church and hoped he might find some guidance at the Bible church down the street. Sure enough, they had a ten-week program with classes and personal counseling sessions. They had notebooks, and every principle they taught was followed by a Scripture verse. Titus felt hope. He went to every class and met with a counselor about five times.

At first, everything was going great. He didn't have a drink, and he stayed away from porn for almost two months. But then, one Friday, he saw his ex-wife and the kids at the park. He froze. He wasn't sure what to do. They had a friendly yet awkward conversation, and he went home.

He decided to do an internet search on a toy for one of the kids, and a picture on the side caught his eye. In a moment of weakness, he clicked on the image and everything inside went numb. He never went to sleep that night. He just binged all the porn he could find. Feeling like he had hit rock bottom anyway, he also got smashed.

Titus never went back to the Bible church. He felt too much shame. For a few months, he went back to his old lifestyle until he once again thought, *I've got to turn my life around. I can't keep living like this.* This time he went to the Pentecostal church down the street. At the end of the service, they invited anyone who was struggling with sin or anyone who needed a miracle to come down to the altar. Well, Titus needed both, so he went forward. People laid hands on him and something amazing happened. He felt a rush of energy surge through his body, and the next thing he knew, he was waking up to people praying and speaking in tongues as he lay on the floor.

This church also took him in. They had people who agreed to meet with him. They commanded the spirits of alcohol and porn to leave, and they prayed that he would receive the baptism of the Holy Spirit. Once again, Titus felt hope. The knowledge and advice he got at the Bible church had been good, but it lacked power. Now that he had Holy Spirit power, he was sure his battle was over.

A few months into his time at the church, he noticed that the primary solutions they seemed to offer were to come back to the altar and go through a fresh anointing or a fresh deliverance. He was starting to stall, and it scared him. Then something really unexpected happened. He fell in love.

There was a beautiful girl in the church who had issues of her own. Her name was Lisa. She was also divorced and, from the sound of things, her husband had been a monster. Titus found himself wanting to rescue this beauty and start a new life with her. After all, she "got him." Lisa knew what it was like to be flawed and struggle with temptation. In fact, they started having sex about the same time they began volunteering to help with the children's ministry. They rationalized the sex by saying, "We've both been married before. The rules aren't the same for us. People can't expect us to wait."

Eventually, word reached the church elders about their indiscretion, and they were disciplined in a way that made them decide to leave the church altogether. A month later, Lisa left Titus, and he went into a very dark place. From what Titus could see, the church really didn't have any answers to his problems. He became disillusioned with Christianity and dropped out of the church scene completely.

This story may be depressing, but it is all too common. Titus and Lisa are composite characters from people I have known, but I have heard stories like this dozens of times. People often look to the church for solutions to their problems only to leave disillusioned—or worse, traumatized. I know too many people who never want to attend church again because of how their problems were handled.

From a maturity development perspective, Titus represents someone stuck at infant-level maturity. Guys like Titus often want to be a hero to the people in their lives. Titus likely wanted to be a hero to his kids and a hero to Lisa, but he lacked the emotional capacity to follow through on those desires. As long as he was seen as a hero—whether to his family or the people trying to help him—he flourished. But when he couldn't be the hero, he fell into an emotional pit that turned him into a different person who saw life differently and followed different values. The part of him that wanted to be a good Christian and strong spiritual leader disappeared, and the part of him that just wanted to feel better took over. I have talked to a lot of guys who were trying to break a cycle of addiction and most of them will tell you that they go into a different space in their head while they are drinking, doing drugs, or watching porn, and when they are done and feeling like themselves again, they think to themselves, *Who was that? How did I turn into that person?*

While Titus was an emotional infant, Lisa was an emotional child. She represents someone who missed the life experiences she needed in order to form a clear identity and strong skills in emotional regulation. As a child, she could ask for what she needed, but to someone like Titus, that sounded a lot like nagging. Because of some painful experiences in her past, Lisa also tended to be controlling. She made vows never to feel that kind of pain again, so she tried to control her world in a way that would protect her from pain.

When you get an emotional infant and an emotional child together, they may genuinely love each other, but without some maturity development, the relationship is going to be rocky and either volatile or passive. In a volatile relationship, people constantly bicker and routinely blow up at each other. In a passive relationship, people avoid each other. They stay together, but their lives don't overlap much. Some couples bounce back and forth between the two styles. They spend a lot of time avoiding each other because, when they do interact, it either goes well or it goes badly.

The reality is that people like Titus and Lisa can do well in spurts, but until they fill the holes in their maturity development, they will be locked into a cycle of frustrating relationships and addictive behaviors.

BUILDING A MATURITY DEVELOPMENT PLAN

Having defined our goal as maturity, we need a plan to reach that goal. Let me start by introducing five essential strategies for freedom, healing, and wholeness. Then, I'll take some time to explain how I got there. You can remember the five strategies of this plan with the acronym BUILD, which makes sense because the goal is to build maturity:

B – Be aware of your body.
U – Unleash your beliefs.
I – Increase the joy in your bonds.
L – Listen to the Spirit.
D – Deal with demons.

These five strategies form a growth model based on the idea that there are five engines that drive our emotions. Three of these engines are physical: our bodies, our beliefs, and our bonds. Two of the engines are spiritual: the Holy Spirit and wicked spirits. Let's take a quick look at the engines and how they lead us to the strategies embodied in the acronym BUILD.

Engine 1: Our Bodies

Every emotion we feel is also experienced by our bodies. For example, when we get sad, we lose energy and may involuntarily find ourselves tearing up or letting our shoulders droop. Fear can make our faces hot, our hearts race, our hands shake, our knees quake, and our stomachs tighten up in knots. Anger can literally make us see red as the capillaries behind our eyes burst under pressure. Despair can drain our energy so that we don't want to get out of bed or move from our chair. We feel emotions in our bodies, and we express them with our bodies.

When it comes to the connection between our bodies and our emotions, the traffic runs in two directions. First, it can run from our bodies to our emotions. This happens when activity in our bodies drive our emotions. For example, the release of dopamine or adrenaline will have a significant effect on how we feel. When we lack sleep, work too much, get injured, or have an illness, the problems in our bodies will impact the way we feel. This is the body driving the way we feel.

Second, the traffic can run from our emotions to our bodies. While in a doctor's office for an appointment, I asked the doctor if he thought a lot of the problems he saw were rooted in emotions and negative thinking. Almost immediately, he responded that he believed 80 percent of the physical problems he helped his patients manage were rooted in emotional issues. Books like *The Body Keeps the Score* by renowned trauma expert Bessel van der Kolk have shined a spotlight on the impact of emotional trauma on the body's ability to function well. It only makes sense that if our bodies are run down by shame and despair or amped up with anxiety and anger, these emotions will eventually take a toll on our bodies.

The Bible often highlights the connection between our emotions and our bodies. For example, in Daniel 5:6, we read that when King

Belshazzar saw God's hand appear and write on the wall of his palace, "he was so frightened that his legs became weak and his knees were knocking." Notice that his internal emotions were expressed involuntarily through his body's response.

The Bible also emphasizes the relationship between our emotions and our hearts. For instance, when Joseph's brothers realized his "stolen" cup was in Benjamin's bag, the text says, "their hearts sank" (Gen. 42:28). The image of a heart sinking reflects the reality that despair sucks the energy out of our bodies and makes us want to stop what we are doing and give up. Interestingly, this verse also mentions that the brothers felt fear that caused trembling in their bodies.

Despair and fear are opposite emotions but often linked. Despair is a low-energy emotion that sucks the life out of our bodies. Fear is a high-energy emotion that produces trembling. In the case of Joseph's brothers, both were happening at the same time. They felt despair at their hopeless situation and also fear at what the consequences might be. A combination of emotions like this is hard on the body. Despair is like stepping on the emotional brakes, and fear is like stepping on the emotional gas. When we do both at the same time, it is easy to see how it could cause significant physical problems.

Engine #1 leads directly to Strategy #1 in our plan for developing maturity: Be aware of our bodies. Whether it is starting to notice how our emotions are affecting our bodies or taking steps to make lifestyle changes that affect our bodies, some breakthroughs can only take place by being aware of the role that our bodies play.

Engine #2: Our Beliefs (Left Brain)

There is little question that what we believe can drive how we feel. When we believe we are worthless, it makes us feel shame. When we believe we have been wronged, it makes us feel anger. When we believe we are in danger, it makes us feel fear.

My father used to say he wanted to write a book called *Believe Right, Live Right*. His premise was that people don't always practice what they say they believe, but they always practice what they really believe. He knew that what we believe drives the way we feel and act, so he wanted to help people get to the root issues and find breakthrough by changing their beliefs.

There is a lot of truth to the idea that changing our beliefs will change our emotions. We likely all have stories of getting really angry about something only to find out later that we were mistaken and there was no need to get angry. This happens because our emotions can't tell the difference between true and false beliefs. This is a common experience. I remember getting really scared when I thought a burglar was trying to break in to our home. I was in junior high and had some friends over when I saw a shadowy figure trying to open a window on the second floor of our house. I ran downstairs and saw a strange car in the driveway, which confirmed my fear. However, it turned out that the "burglar" was my older brother. The car belonged to a friend of his, and he was on the roof trying to find an open door because he was locked out of the house, and my friends and I were making too much noise to hear him ringing the doorbell! My emotions were convinced of a narrative that turned out to be false. This is why I say that our emotions can't tell fact from fiction, and if we rely solely on our emotions to determine what is true, they will often mislead us.

Identifying false beliefs and replacing them with the truth is an important and powerful engine for changing our emotions and behavior. It is such a clear solution. However, we can be tempted to make it the only solution. Yet, as important as beliefs are, I believe the next engine—our bonding—is an even more powerful factor than beliefs in driving how we feel.

Engine #2 leads directly to Strategy #2: Unleashing our beliefs. I think unleashing is a good word for what is happening here because beliefs will either enslave us or set us free. If we want to unleash new hope for an abundant life, we need to unleash our beliefs and anchor our world in truth.

Engine #3: Our Bonds (Right Brain)

The deepest part of our brain activity is related to attachment. God designed us so that we process life's experiences in a part of our brain that operates faster than conscious thought. This means that before we ever get a chance to form a belief about something, we have already had an emotional reaction to situations we face.

For instance, if an old friend suddenly showed up at my front door, I would feel all sorts of emotions inside before I ever formulated a coherent thought about what was going on. I might instinctively feel joy and the high-energy excitement of an unexpected pleasure. Or, I might feel anxiety without being sure exactly why I am feeling that way. As I stop and think about it, I might remember that our last interaction didn't go well, but I felt the emotion before the belief was present. Depending on several factors, I might feel anger, fear, shame, sadness, disgust, despair, or joy when someone from my past shows up unexpectedly. These emotions show up at a deeper level of my brain than the part of my brain that thinks with words and forms beliefs.

In terms of brain function, cravings are anchored in the attachment apparatus on the right side of the brain. These cravings drive our desire for attachment. What our brains really want is someone who is happy to be with us, or for a specific person to be happy to be with us. We have all seen a small child crying for their mother. No one else would do; it had to be mom. When the attachment we crave is not possible, we feel pain. It can be a mild pain because someone simply isn't home at the moment. Or it can be the deep pain of longing for connection with someone who is emotionally or physically unavailable.

For example, when I was young, I fell in love more times than I care to admit. Every time I fell in love, no one else would satisfy my longing. I had to be with that particular person. I spent a lot of emotional energy pining over girls who didn't want to be with me and even went through a period of depression when one girl broke my heart just as I was starting seminary. Now that I have been happily married to the same woman for over thirty years, I look back with relief that those other relationships didn't work out. But at the time, the craving center in my brain was sure I would die if I couldn't be with that particular person.

Our craving for joyful attachment is a powerful driver of emotions. Fear, anger, shame, sadness, despair, and disgust are all deep emotional reactions to something misfiring when it comes to our attachments. These attachment-based emotions impact us physically before we ever have a chance to think clearly about what is going on. In fact, we often form wrong beliefs about our experiences because the part of our brain that forms beliefs does not have access to all of the data.

There is a reason why we often struggle with emotions without knowing what has triggered them. They are being triggered at a deep place in the brain that conscious thought can't access. Thus, when I was pining over girls who didn't want to be with me, I formed beliefs based on my attachment pain. Those beliefs made my problem worse. I believed things like, "She is the only one who can make me happy," "My life is meaningless without her," and "If God won't make this work out, how can I trust Him?" The brain can go in some weird directions when attachment pain is driving the show.

As I have learned more about attachment theory, it has caused me to go back to the Bible and take a closer look at what it says. Not surprisingly, the Bible has a lot to say about belonging and attachment. However, many of us have been so anchored in the voluntarist idea that beliefs and choices explain everything that we miss the role of attachment in the text. Our voluntarist worldview serves as a filter that blocks out what it doesn't know to look for.

Let's look at a concept like love. My training taught me to think of love as a choice. I remember preaching that the description of love in 1 Corinthians 13 was basically a checklist of choices we ought to make in order to be more loving people. It made sense:

Choose to be patient.
Choose to be kind.
Choose not to envy.

Choose not to be boastful.

Choose not to be arrogant, rude, self-seeking, etc.

Only recently did I realize I was reducing love to a series of choices and missing the role of attachment in love. If I don't like you and don't want a relationship with you but choose to be kind anyway, do I love you or am I just trying to do what is right? Isn't love something more than choosing to behave a certain way despite how you feel?

For example, when Jesus forgave those who were crucifying Him, was He thinking, *I really can't stand you, but because it is the right thing to do, I will choose to forgive you?* Or did He love these people? Did He have a desire for attachment with them? Did He choose to forgive them simply out of duty, or did the forgiveness spring from love, which is actually much deeper than a mere choice?

One of the core lessons neuroscience has helped me see is that there are only two types of bonds the brain can form: a *joy bond* and a *fear bond.* A joy bond sends hormones like dopamine and oxytocin to the control center of our brains. It gives a high-energy feeling we call joy—knowing we are happy to be with someone and they are happy to be with us. A fear bond sends hormones like cortisol through our system and either causes a negative energy spike—like fear and anger—or a negative energy crash such as despair, shame, disgust, and sadness. If our brain has learned to bond to others in joy, it is easier to regulate our emotions and act like ourselves. But when we have learned to bond in fear, our brain amplifies fear, leading to all sorts of disorders and dysfunctions.

Let's pause for a moment and review the first three engines that are related to the body and the brain. You can remember these engines with the words body, beliefs, and bonds. The picture below is meant to highlight the idea that beliefs are related to the left brain, bonds to the right brain, and the body connects it all.

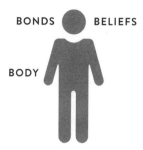

BONDS BELIEFS

BODY

As we turn to the spirit world, there are two primary engines: the Holy Spirit (God) and wicked spirits (demons). I hesitated calling these "engines" because both the Holy Spirit and wicked spirits are personal entities, not just forces, and I didn't want people to get the wrong idea. In the end, I went with engines because both the Holy Spirit and wicked spirits can impact all three physical engines. They are emotional and behavioral drivers that we often overlook.

Engine #3 points us directly to Strategy #3: Increasing your joy bonds. The life change that can happen by learning to transform fear bonds into joy bonds is hard to overstate. When joy becomes the fuel that drives our lives and our brains learn to amplify joy rather than fear, the foundation for life shifts dramatically.

Engine #4: The Holy Spirit

Clearly, God's Spirit can have a profound impact on our bodies, our beliefs, and our attachments. When it comes to bonding, the Hebrew Scriptures encourage us to love God with all our hearts (Deut. 6:5) and to walk with Him in humility (Mic. 6:8). In the New Testament, we are urged to "keep in step with the Spirit" (Gal. 5:25), which is not just about obeying a superior, it is about developing an intimate relationship. The idea of a deeper walk is inseparable from walking in the Spirit.

The Holy Spirit is a person, not a force, so when I say the Holy Spirit is an engine, it is because the Spirit plays a significant role in driving our emotions and behaviors. As I read the Bible, I see three primary ways the Holy Spirit impacts our lives:

1. **Presence.** God is enthroned in heaven, yet He is also present in my heart. This is only possible because the Spirit of God lives in all who believe. It is because of the Holy Spirit that I can say I am never alone. God is always with me.

2. **Wisdom.** The Spirit is the source of all wisdom. In Exodus 31:3, we read that Bezalel was filled with the Spirit of God and thus had wisdom, understanding, knowledge, and skill. In the same way, when we are filled with the Spirit, He gives us the wisdom to avoid what is evil and do what is good (Eph. 5:18–20).

3. **Power.** The Holy Spirit is the source of miraculous power. Thus, Paul could write that he did not preach the gospel to the Corinthians with merely human wisdom, but with a demonstration of the Spirit's power (1 Cor. 2:4).

When it comes to our healing journey, there are two crucial ways in which the Spirit is involved. The first is through a lifestyle of attention to the Spirit's leading. As people develop a lifestyle of listening prayer, they deepen their walk with God and benefit from His wisdom. The second is through His power. There are times when God performs miracles and brings healing through the presence and power of His Spirit.

Engine #4 points us to Strategy #4: Listening to the Spirit. It should come as no surprise that walking in the Spirit is one of the keys to breakthrough. If we live in the flesh, what hope do we have? But if we learn to walk in the Spirit and develop the discernment to recognize His voice, we form a relationship with a God who is happy to see us and available to us twenty-four hours a day, seven days a week.

Engine #5: Wicked Spirits

The Bible teaches a spiritual warfare worldview. From the opening pages of Genesis through the concluding pages of Revelation, the world of the Bible is a world inhabited by spirits—both angelic and demonic. Just as the Holy Spirit can impact our bodies, beliefs, and bonds, so wicked spirits can affect each of these engines. Demons can affect the body. They are lying spirits who serve the father of lies (John 8:44). They feed division, envy, and strife, promoting fear rather than shalom (Gal. 5:19–21; James 3:14–16).

Demons are like sharks. They don't see someone bleeding and say, "They are in enough trouble. I'll stay out of it." Most people who have a deep bondage issue like addiction, also have a demonic issue. For some, evicting the demons ends the addiction. For others, it is part of the process.

Engine #5 leads us to Strategy #5: Dealing with demons. A lot of Western Christians have a very underdeveloped understanding of spiritual warfare. We may think it only applies to people in other countries or those engaging in witchcraft. But spiritual warfare is an everyday part of life for all of us. It is not an elective in the Christian life that we can opt out of. The good news is that there are concrete skills we can develop that can help us live in victory over the work of the enemy and find freedom from demonic strongholds.

When you bring them together, these five engines help us understand the sort of strategies we will need in order to experience the breakthroughs we hope to see. In the chapters ahead, we will take a deeper look at the growth model created by these engines and the specific strategies they require.

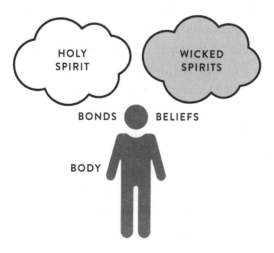

BUILD MATURITY

As we have seen, recognizing these five engines leads us to five strategies for building maturity. Thus, this growth model can be called the BUILD Maturity Model. It identifies maturity as the "product" we are trying to build, and you can think of the five engines as the "factory" designed to produce that product. Here is a quick summary of these five strategies.

B—*Be Aware of Your Body (Engine 1)*

When it comes to our emotional health, we can sometimes forget how much impact our bodies have. However, whether it is adequate sleep, proper diet and exercise, or meditation and quieting exercises, we need to pay attention to the role our body plays in driving our emotions.

U—*Unleash True Beliefs (Engine 2)*

Toxic thinking can drive us into dark places. False thinking can guide us into foolish decisions. Correcting our thought life can unleash a transformational power that has helped many people experience a breakthrough.

I—*Increase Your Joy Bonds (Engine 3)*

Filling the holes in our maturity development requires learning how to reprogram the way we form attachments from fear to joy. Joy bonds create belonging. Belonging creates identity. Identity drives the way we live. Increasing our joy bonds requires improving our relational skills and developing tools for emotional regulation.

L—*Listen to the Spirit (Engine 4)*

Both the healing of painful memories and intimacy in our walk with God require the practice of listening prayer. In order to grow our maturity, we need to learn the difference between walking in the flesh and walking in the Spirit. Developing intimacy with God through spiritual disciplines and listening prayer is essential to that process.

D—*Defeat Demons (Engine 5)*

We are in a war whether we know it or not. It is important to learn how the enemy works and what we need in order to defeat him. Whether it is taking thoughts captive or evicting wicked spirits, spiritual warfare is essential to tearing down the strongholds that keep us in bondage.

REVISITING TITUS AND LISA

When I think back on the dozens of couples who have come to me for marital help through the years, a lot of those couples fit the core pattern of a man stuck at infant-level maturity and a woman functioning at child-level maturity who were trying to raise kids. It was a recipe for disaster. I often heard men privately complain that their wives were controlling, angry people who had forgotten how to have fun. I heard the wives complain that they wished their husbands would grow up and take some responsibility so they didn't feel like it all fell on them. Raising kids meant they were both trapped in a life that kept them living on the edge of their emotional capacity. As a result, passivity and volatility reigned, and the kids usually grew up to be teens who couldn't wait to get out of the house.

The bright spot in all of this was that a maturity model gave these couples a path to follow. It explained what was going on and why they felt the way they did. It also helped me know that I couldn't give them everything they needed in a counseling setting. Some of this was going to require group work, some of it biblical counseling, some of it prayer ministry, and some of it the development of new habits.

More than once I have had a Titus or a Lisa come to my office for help and start a journey that led to someplace beautiful. It often started with listening prayer that helped them connect to God in a meaningful way, or spiritual warfare that got them free from some level of compulsion or oppression, but the ones who really took off were the ones who connected with others and went on the journey together. Many of these people started as emotional infants and grew to become true adults, parents, and elders.

The rest of this book will unpack the BUILD Maturity Model. In the next chapter, we will take a closer look at what maturity is by exploring the brain science and attachment theory that help us understand it.

CHAPTER 4

MATURITY AND THE BRAIN

WHEN I WAS THE SENIOR PASTOR of a community church in Indiana, someone encouraged me to read a book about maturity called *The Life Model: Living from the Heart Jesus Gave You.*[1] Partway through the book, there was a chart that identified the characteristics of people who were stuck at infant- or child-level maturity. I remember that experience well because I had an "aha" moment as I realized I was largely functioning at child-level maturity while trying to do an elder-level job. The gap was pretty obvious and explained why I felt overwhelmed so much of the time.

As I began to learn everything I could about maturity and the brain science related to it, it became increasingly clear that my child-level maturity was having a negative impact on my marriage too. In fact, if you talk to my wife, she will tell you that discovering *The Life Model* and learning to identify missing relational skills was the turning point in our marriage. Before that, my wife felt neglected. She felt like she always got the scraps and that my best effort went to the church first and then to my own care second. I thought she was overreacting, but it turns out she wasn't. That is just what it feels like to be married to an emotional child.

One of the lessons I learned was that immature people often shut down when they get overwhelmed. Two of the key indicators of emotional maturity are the ability to remain relational and act like yourself when emotions get triggered. I decided to pay attention to how I did in that department. As it turned out, it didn't take much for me to shut down completely. One day, my wife used a critical tone of voice with me, and that was all it took. I suddenly stopped talking and went into a dark place in my mind I later described as my "man cave." It was where I went when life got hard to try and disappear for a while. Instead of acting like myself—a mature Christian leader—I acted like a five-year-old. It was a real wake-up call as I realized that most of the relational and emotional problems I had could be traced in one way or another back to holes in my maturity.

EMOTIONAL CAPACITY

Maturity can be measured in terms of *emotional capacity*. For example, we expect parents to be able to handle more distress than teens and teens to be able to handle more hardship than children and children to be able to handle their emotions with greater skill than infants. At each stage of maturity, we expect people to have greater capacity to deal with their emotions.

Emotional capacity refers to how much pressure you can handle before you blow up, shut down, or melt down. Daniel Siegel describes emotional capacity as our "window of tolerance."[2] The idea can be illustrated with your hand. Your thumb represents the lower part of your brain where our cravings are and our "fight or flight" reactions occur. Your other four fingers represent the top part of your brain that regulates emotions and remembers who we are and how to act like ourselves.

When you wrap your thumb with your other four fingers and make a fist, this represents a brain that is functioning well so that each part of the brain is able to stay connected to the other parts. As long as our emotional stress level stays within our window of tolerance, our brain operates normally. However, if we get triggered—if we suddenly have to face emotions that are bigger than our capacity—we experience something Siegel calls "flipping the lid."[3] To illustrate this, imagine that your fist suddenly opens so that all of your fingers are spread out. Your thumb is no longer in contact with the other fingers. In the same way, when we get triggered and pushed beyond our capacity, we lose access to the higher-level brain functions that help us regulate our emotions. We suddenly find ourselves outside of our window of tolerance dealing with a level of emotion we have no capacity to tolerate. When this happens, our relational self disappears. It is just like when I lost my ability to act like myself when I got triggered by my wife's tone of voice.

SHALOM

When we live within our emotional capacity, we feel peace. Crazy things may be happening all around us, but in the center of the storm, we are at peace because we have not been pushed beyond our capacity to handle what is going on. The Hebrew word for this kind of peace is *shalom*. We experience shalom when we know we are with someone who can handle what is happening. When they are not overwhelmed, it helps us not to be overwhelmed. You can think of this as being with someone with a "bigger brain."[4]

When I think of a "bigger brain," I picture a little boy or girl who has a nightmare and runs to their mom and dad's room. Sometimes just being in the presence of a safe person with a bigger brain helps. I can remember sneaking into my parents' room as a kid after having a nightmare. I didn't even have to wake them up in order to feel peace. I knew that if I needed them, someone would be there who could take care of me. These two components—knowing we are not alone and that we are going to be okay—are essential to remaining within our window of tolerance.

Throughout the Bible, we see God offering His presence and His "bigger brain" as comfort for whatever we have to endure. When Israel was on the verge of entering Canaan, they were afraid. They were about to face some of their greatest fears—attacking a land filled with giants— and they were going to do it without Moses because he was "no longer able to lead" them (Deut. 31:2). To encourage them with this challenge, Moses offered them two sources of comfort:

1. Moses told them they would not be alone. The same God who had brought them out of Egypt, provided for them in the desert, and destroyed powerful armies led by the giants Sihon and Og would go with them. They would also not be alone because the experienced leader and warrior Joshua would take the mantle from Moses and fill his role as shepherd.

2. Moses told them they would be successful. Victory had been promised. Possession of the land was promised, and God's promises always came through. They were going to be okay. Thus he could say, "Do not be afraid or terrified because of them [the giant-filled nations they had to fight], for [Yahweh] your God goes with you; he will never leave you nor forsake you" (Deut. 31:6).

Moses also comforted Joshua and helped him stay within his window of tolerance. In front of the entire congregation, Moses told him, "Be strong and courageous, for you must go with this people into the land that [Yahweh] swore to their [forefathers] to give them [a reminder that everything was going to be okay], and you must divide it among them as their inheritance. [Yahweh] himself goes before you and will be with you [so you are not alone]; he will never leave you nor forsake you. Do not be afraid; do not be discouraged" (Deut. 31:7–8).

THREE KEY FACTS ABOUT THE BRAIN

In our book *Rare Leadership in the Workplace*, Jim Wilder and I identify a few essential facts about the brain that help us understand its role in maturity development. I'll recap them briefly here.

1. The Brain Craves the Fuel of Joy[5]

The brain wants to run on the fuel of joy. When it does, it runs smoothly and efficiently. It hums like a finely tuned engine and can be thought of as running cool because it is not under stress and is well within its capacity to handle what it needs to do. If the brain can't find joy, it will run on fear. Over time, fear causes all sorts of problems in the brain. It will run hot as it is constantly taxed trying to manage everything it needs to control. By staying constantly on the edge of our emotional capacity and frequently pushing ourselves beyond that edge, we find it easier to shut down, blow up, or melt down. We have a shorter fuse. Living with fear as our primary fuel will also put stress on our bodies and cause all sorts of physical problems to develop.

Joy keeps us in the front of our brains; fear pushes activity to the back of the brain. Running on the fuel of joy and operating in the front of our brains are synonyms. Running on the fuel of fear and getting trapped in the back of our brains are also parallel ideas.

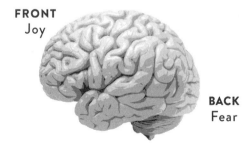

FRONT
Joy

BACK
Fear

2. Brain Activity Flows from Right to Left

Our brains are designed with two hemispheres that mirror each other. The right hemisphere of the brain is the primary home of the social systems related to relationships and emotional regulation. The left hemisphere of the brain is the primary home of our problem-solving abilities. It is where we analyze, strategize, and explain. The left hemisphere of the brain cannot do relationships. We don't think our way into attachment. Attachment is a right hemisphere experience.

The right side of the brain deals with our experiences at a level that is faster than conscious thought. This means that before our left brain has a chance to form a narrative about something or make a decision about it, our right brain has already processed the data and decided how much of it to pass on and how we feel about it.

Our experience of the world around us comes first to the right hemisphere of the brain and then moves to the left. Not the other way around. This means that if something is wrong on the right side of the brain, it will affect what happens on the left side. If I am in emotional distress, I don't tend to make my best decisions or do my best thinking.

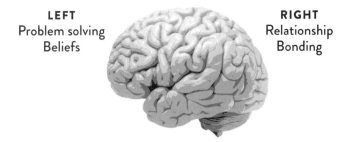

LEFT
Problem solving
Beliefs

RIGHT
Relationship
Bonding

3. The Brain Functions in Levels[6]

There are four primary levels of brain function in the right hemisphere of the brain. These can be thought of as a "joy elevator" with stops at all four floors. When everything is working smoothly, we naturally move from the first floor to the top floor several times each second, which keeps our command center at the top in charge of our lives. However, if something goes wrong and the elevator gets stuck, we lose access to our higher-level brain function, which keeps us from remaining relational or acting like ourselves.

The four levels of the brain (or the four elevator floors) are attachment, assessment, attunement, and action. I will explain these more fully later in the book. For now, it is important to understand that problems at lower levels of our brain affect higher-level brain functions and affect the way our left brain processes the problems it tries to solve.

4 – ACTION (JOY/IDENTITY)

3 – ATTUNEMENT

2 – ASSESSMENT

1 – ATTACHMENT

The following image of the brain, developed by Dr. Jim Wilder, shows more accurately where a lot of this activity is occurring.[7]

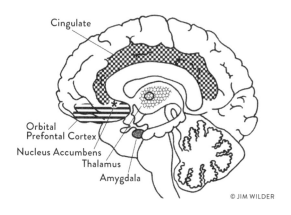

Cingulate

Orbital
Prefontal Cortex
Nucleus Accumbens
Thalamus
Amygdala

© JIM WILDER

The attachment center of the brain is primarily composed of the thalamus and the nucleus accumbens near the center of the brain that is closest to where the spine connects. The assessment center basically is the amygdala, which serves as something of a guard shack at a border crossing to assess whether what is trying to pass is good, bad, or scary. The attunement center is the cingulate, and, in this picture, it is relatively large and shaped a bit like a banana. This is the part of the brain that reads people and our environment. It is like radar that is constantly running. The fourth level is the action center. It is the part of the brain I have referred to as the joy center or the identity center. In this diagram, it is called the orbital prefrontal cortex. I will have a lot more to say about these levels of the brain in the chapter on bonding.

TWO ESSENTIAL BRAIN DEVELOPMENTS

When babies are first born, most of the brain structure they will need in order to regulate their emotions, act like themselves, and live with maturity are completely undeveloped. These brain structures will only grow through relational interaction. Without the interaction they need, infants will not develop an integrated self. In other words, they will not be able to regulate their emotions in a way that allows them to maintain a core identity. Instead, they will create pseudo-identities for every emotion they feel. A pseudo-identity is one we create on the left side of our brain in order to solve a problem, limit damage, or make sure we win. There are a lot of terms for this. We call it wearing a mask, posing, putting on an act, or pretending to be someone we are not. The point is that we are not being our true self.

Maturity is directly related to living as a whole-brained person. It means we are able to keep our higher-level brain functions engaged even when we are under emotional stress. If there are holes in our maturity development, it often manifests in some of the following ways:

1. An inability to remain relational when things get hard. Instead we blow up, shut down, or melt down.
2. An inability to regulate or quiet from our emotions. Instead we live with a high degree of emotional instability. We often get stuck in our upset emotions so that they take over our lives.
3. An inability to act like ourselves under pressure. Instead we "wear a mask" or present a false front hoping it will get us what we want in whatever situation we are facing.
4. An inability to say no to ourselves. We have trouble working for and waiting for what we need. Instead we live for temporary pleasures and often find ourselves battling addiction.

Our emotional capacity is directly related to two areas of growth in the brain. First, it is related to the size of our joy center. Second, it is related to the strength of our joy pathways. Here is a brief explanation.

Our Joy Center

The command center of the brain is technically called the right orbital prefrontal cortex.[8] It serves as both the identity center and the joy center of the brain. The implications of this are profound. God designed us so that our core identity would be anchored in joy (not fear) and so that our joyful, relational self should be in charge. God did not want our overwhelmed, scared, angry, or discouraged self running the show.

One of the key tasks (perhaps *the* key task) of infant development is the formation of an integrated self. An integrated self is simply a core identity that doesn't fall apart under stress. As previously mentioned, when a baby is born, most of the hardware in the brain related to identity and emotional regulation is undeveloped. This is why relational interactions with others are so important in the early years of life. All of these interactions serve as workouts that determine how the brain grows and organizes itself in terms of how we see ourselves and our place in this world.

Our joy center is located above our right eye and is the control center of the relational part of our brain. It remembers who we are and how it is like us to act. When this part of the brain is underdeveloped, we will have problems. We will not be able to act like ourselves under stress. Thus, a different part of our brain creates a false self that takes over when we get triggered. That false self may be cocky and self-assured. Or it may be angry, or childish, or manipulative, or any number of other alternative forms of ourselves.

To picture how a false self gets formed, I think of a little girl who comes downstairs for breakfast and asks to have some super sugary cereal. Mom immediately says no, but dad doesn't say anything. The girl starts going through her options of what strategy is most likely to get her what she wants. She might try charm. She might snuggle up next to mom, make her eyes really big, and look as cute as possible to see if that will break mom's will so she gets what she wants. If that works, it becomes part of the arsenal she will use the rest of her life to get what she wants. If that doesn't work, the little girl might throw a fit, or attempt a divide-and-conquer strategy by recruiting dad to her side. There are hundreds of ways she can try to take control of the situation in order to get what she wants. To the extent that any of these work, she is on her way to developing a false self.

People also develop a false self in order to protect themselves from pain. The more secure I feel in a relationship, the safer I feel in acting like myself. But the less secure the relationship, the more fear will drive me to act like the person I think I need to be in order to survive the situation. For example, if the little girl has asked for sugary breakfast cereal before and got yelled at, shamed, and made to feel fear, the main lesson she learns is that her parents can be scary and have to be managed carefully. Instead of functioning from the control center of her brain and acting like herself, she goes into the problem-solving, damage control part of her brain and lives out of the false self she has learned will give her the best chance of surviving such experiences.

Our joy center is largely unformed at birth. It grows and develops as we interact with other people. Thus relational interaction is essential to the development of our identity. If we get lots of joyful smiles and if people notice our needs and meet them quickly, we develop a stable sense of self and a core conviction that people generally like us. If we don't get many joyful smiles, and if people don't notice our needs or respond to them in life-giving ways, our joy center will not develop properly. Fear will play a greater role than joy in forming our sense of self and shape the unwritten rules by which we live. Instead of developing a core conviction that people like us, we will tend to assume there is something wrong with us and that we must perform in order to get people to treat us well.

When our joy center is highly developed, we will have a very stable sense of identity, a clear set of core values, and a high ability to live with joy despite experiencing big emotions we may feel. However, an underdeveloped joy center forces us to live from a place of fear and the command center of the brain will often go offline to let the false self manage the situation. When this happens, our relationships will tend to be transactional rather than joyful. We will expect to have to play a role or wear a mask in order to be accepted.

Our Joy Pathways

In addition to a well-developed joy center, we will need fully formed joy pathways if we want to live with high emotional capacity. Joy pathways are built as we recover from upsetting emotions. They help us move our brain function from the false self part of our brain to the joy center.

When we are born, we have no joy pathways in the brain. This is because joy pathways are created as neurons bond together to form bridges from one part of the brain to another that allow us to recover from a variety of emotions. These neural pathways form as we interact relationally with others. We are not born with them already in place. They have to be developed through experience.

Because there are no joy pathways in the brain at birth, we have no ability to keep our joy center (or command center) in charge when we get upset. Joy pathways begin to form when someone notices that we are upset and takes the time to be relationally present with us as we recover.

They will need to validate our emotions by meeting us where we are, comfort us, and help us recover. As people notice when we are upset and go through the relational process of helping us recover, neurons in our brain begin to link together and a path begins to form that helps us recover from that emotion. At first the path will be tiny and fragile, like it was hacked out of the jungle by a machete. But the more often that path gets used, the stronger it gets. It develops into a well-worn walking path that eventually becomes a dirt road.

As traveling that road becomes a habit, the brain begins to wrap the well-developed neural pathway in our brain with white matter. The white matter turns our joy pathway from a well-worn road into a superhighway. White matter processes data at super fast speeds. When our recovery highways have become strong habits, we can recover from upsetting emotions quickly without even thinking about how we did it. In fact, returning to joy from our upsetting emotions can happen so automatically, we can have trouble understanding why it is so hard for others to navigate the same emotions. It feels simple to us.

Add to this the fact that it is possible for people to develop a large joy center and joy pathways wrapped in white matter by the time they are three or four years old and you begin to understand why some people seem to be naturally happy and naturally resilient. They have never really experienced life without these well-developed structures in place. On the other hand, if we get into our childhood years and our joy center is still small and our joy pathways are underdeveloped, life can feel overwhelming. As a result, we will learn to avoid certain emotions because we don't know how to handle them. We will also form addictions to soothe ourselves when we get stuck in emotions our brain hasn't learned how to process.

AN INTEGRATED SELF

As we have seen, the joy center is the home of our true selves. When the joy center is not in control, a false self will take over and run the show.

When the joy center is in control, we feel the most like ourselves and live with greater peace. Joy pathways are the bridges that help us maintain (or recover) access to our command center from the various emotions we feel. Consider the following diagram.

At the top of this diagram is the self. This represents the joy center (or identity center) that remembers who we are and how it is like us to act. Below the self is a ring. This ring serves as the point of connection between the joy center and our various negative emotions. At the bottom of the diagram are six core negative emotions represented by the acronym SADSAD, which stands for shame, anger, disgust, sadness, anxiety, and despair. I'll explain why those emotions are singled out later in the chapter. The lines linking each letter of SADSAD back to the ring represent the joy pathways that link each of those emotions to the ring and back to the self.

OUR SADSAD EMOTIONS

There are six core negative emotions that are intended to protect us from harm, but these emotions also cause pain. That pain is meant to be an alarm system to alert us to something that needs our attention. However, if we get stuck in that pain and can't recover, it creates even more problems. We usually become addicted, avoidant, angry, and anxious.

These six emotions have not been singled out randomly or merely as examples of upsetting emotions. They are the core reactions we have to a triggered amygdala. The amygdala is the assessment center of the brain. All of our attachments and experiences have to pass by this part of our brain to be evaluated (or assessed). As you may remember, the amygdala has only three options when it comes to assessing our experiences. They can be good, bad, or scary. If they are assessed as good, no alarm is sounded and our brain flow continues on as usual. If they are assessed as bad, the amygdala sends out a signal that lowers our energy levels. When something is bad, it triggers the low-energy emotions of shame, sadness, disgust, and despair. If our experiences are assessed as scary, the amygdala sends a high-energy signal to the body that creates either fear or anger. Fear makes us want to get away from danger. Anger makes us want to stop the scary thing that is happening. This high-energy signal is often called our fight or flight response.

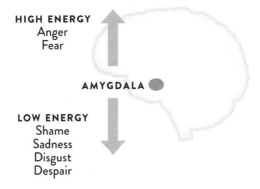

HIGH ENERGY
Anger
Fear

AMYGDALA

LOW ENERGY
Shame
Sadness
Disgust
Despair

I often think of the SADSAD emotions as the color wheel of negative feelings. Nearly every negative emotion we feel can be understood as some combination of these emotions or as some level of how intense these emotions are. For example, frustration would be low-level anger. Rage would be high-level anger. Complex emotions like grief or dread combine several high-intensity elements and are thus more difficult to resolve.

We also need to add one other upsetting emotion to this picture and that is attachment pain. At the deepest levels of our brain function, we find the craving for attachment. When a baby needs mommy, the feeling of attachment pain can reach levels of desperation. When I am in love and cannot be with the person I long to see, I feel attachment pain. The pain of separation can be mild or it can be intense. When attachment pain is added to any of the SADSAD emotions it adds a level of complexity and pain to the experience. With this in mind, here is a brief overview of the SADSAD emotions.

Shame

Shame triggers a nerve in my body which makes me want to hang my head.[9] This emotion becomes toxic when narratives are attached to it that tell us we are bad people. Some people consider all shame as toxic, but this is because they define shame in terms of beliefs. In other words, they start with the bad narratives in their definition. If you define shame as a right-brain emotion that happens at a deeper level than our beliefs, it is not yet toxic. It is an experience that can be resolved in either a toxic or non-toxic way. A non-toxic (healthy) way of dealing with shame is to process it relationally and allow it to become the basis for self-reflection. Without right-brain shame, there is no guilt, no remorse, nothing to cause a person to say, "I was wrong. I'm sorry."

Fear (Anxiety)

Fear is a high-energy emotion that makes us want to get away from pain. Fear is the reaction of the amygdala on the right side of the brain to perceived danger. Anxiety is the reaction of the amygdala on the left side of the brain to imagined danger. If my amygdala has learned that spiders are scary, and I see a spider in my house, the amygdala will trigger a fear reaction before I even have to think about it. On the other hand, if I engage my imagination and wonder, *What if there is a spider in my house?* I can trigger the same sensation of fear even though there is no actual danger.

Disgust

This emotion is related to the impulse to vomit. It is meant to protect us from poisoning ourselves, but can be triggered by anything that makes us feel revulsion. It is not the same as fear, because I am not necessarily afraid of a person or situation that evokes disgust. For example, I may feel disgust when I get a whiff of a smelly diaper or when I smell someone who has been homeless and unwashed for a long period of time. I can feel disgust for an odor without feeling disgust for the person. I remember the first time I gave a ride to someone who had not bathed in a long time. It took weeks for the smell to leave the car. I had to overcome the disgust that odor created in order to act like myself and treat the person with dignity.

Sadness

This low-energy emotion saps the motivation out of us. We feel sad when we lose access to something or someone that brought us joy. Sadness is not the same as attachment pain. We feel attachment pain when we want to connect with someone who is not available. They may be out of the house temporarily, or they may have died, but our desire for an attachment that is not possible creates a deep level of pain. In fact, attachment pain is the deepest pain we can feel. Sadness is more about the loss of what might have been and the loss of someone or something we value.

Anger

Anger is the high-energy emotion that makes me want to stop something painful. It is intended to give me the energy to attack what feels harmful. I can feel this emotion because of what is happening to me or because of what I see happening to someone else.

Despair

This low-energy emotion is related to a feeling of hopelessness. It is triggered by the realization or expectation that I cannot solve my problems with the time and resources at my disposal.

SEPARATE JOY PATHWAYS

We need to develop a separate joy pathway for each of these emotions. It would be nice if we only needed one path from the back of the brain to the front of the brain, but that is not the case. We need a separate path related to each of these six emotions.

If you are looking for a jump start in developing strong joy pathways, you can start quieting and appreciation. Taking five minutes to breathe deeply, tensing and relaxing your muscles, and thinking about something that brings you joy is a great place to begin. Just five minutes two to three times a day can start to grow your capacity for joy in a month or less. There will be more on how to develop skills related to quieting in chapter 6, "Be Aware of Your Body."

For a deeper dive into building emotional capacity, you might want to start with either *The 4 Habits of Joy-Filled People*, which I wrote with Chris Coursey, or *Building Bounce: How to Grow Emotional Resilience*, a book I cowrote with Stefanie Hinman. Both books have a lot of information and practical guidance on how to grow both a large joy center and strong joy pathways.

Hopefully this crash course on the brain and maturity has been helpful in giving you a paradigm for thinking about maturity as the goal of the emotional healing process. Sometimes we read the Bible with a filter that keeps us from recognizing elements of what it teaches. One of the values of understanding the way the brain operates is that it can give us a new perspective on what the Bible teaches. Recognizing that God designed the brain to crave attachment and to run on joy helps us appreciate how deeply God desires to share joy with us.

Our goal is not just relief. It is even more than damage repair. It is building maturity, which will be the focus of the next chapter.

CHAPTER 5

MATURITY DEVELOPMENT ISSUES

SEVERAL YEARS AGO, two different women called our church to ask to meet about issues that had them stuck.[1] They both went through basically the same prayer process with me. I walked each of them through several listening prayer exercises and both dealt with some spiritual warfare issues. Each woman left her session feeling some relief. However, this is where the similarity ends. The first person went on her way and lived with great freedom. Her life was changed in a profound way so that years later, she still looked back on that experience as her "breakthrough" moment. The second person came back to see me a few days later, and she was in greater distress than when we met the first time. Why did the same process for similar problems result in such totally different outcomes? The answer comes down to one word—capacity.

The first woman had been raised in a relatively healthy home, had many good Christian friends, knew the Bible well, and had developed a lot of good habits throughout her life. She primarily needed help opening a door in her heart that had been jammed because of a single traumatic moment in her past. The other woman had grown up with horrific abuse. She had literally been tortured as a child and developed multiple personalities. She missed out on all sorts of developmental skills and had lived her life as a victim, just trying to survive a brutal life. She had almost no friends and lived with a lot of rejection. The first woman had a great deal of emotional capacity, so experiencing a breakthrough set her free to live a full life. The second woman had almost no emotional capacity. Even though she experienced a breakthrough in one small area, she had a hundred other issues that needed to be addressed and enormous holes in her maturity development that needed to be filled.

It is not fair to suggest that a simple prayer session will have the same impact on both of these women. They came into the sessions at completely different maturity levels and with completely different resources for dealing with life. One of the problems with a one-size fits all approach to emotional healing is that people can be all over the place in terms of their maturity and emotional capacity. Some people are stuck because they missed out on all the good stuff they needed in order to thrive. Others are stuck because there is one issue or one traumatic memory that needs resolution. The journey to breakthrough is going to look very different for these two people.

RARE: THE FOUR HABITS OF MATURE PEOPLE

In our book *Rare Leadership*, Jim Wilder and I describe the four habits of mature people. At the heart of these four habits is the idea that mature people are characterized by their ability to suffer well. In other words, they have developed the emotional capacity to experience hardship without losing access to their higher-level brain functions. Mature people have the ability to keep the joy center in command even when difficult situations trigger difficult emotions.[2]

When our joy elevator is consistently able to reach the top floor, it allows us to remain relational and act like ourselves. When big emotions temporarily stall the elevator, mature adults are able to recognize the problem and take steps to return to joy. Let's take a closer look at the four habits that characterize adult maturity.

Habit 1: Remain Relational

The attachment system on the right side of our brains is filled with relational circuitry. When our relational circuits are on, it is easy for us to access our higher-level brain functions. These higher-level functions allow us to remain relational and act like ourselves. When our relational circuits dim or shut down completely, we can lose our ability to remain relational. Instead, we go into problem-solving mode and start treating people like problems to solve. And no one likes being treated like a problem to solve.

We can tell if our relational circuits are offline with one core test—curiosity. I can tell my relational circuits are on when I am curious about what the other person thinks and feels. If I lose my curiosity, it means my relational circuits are off. If someone is talking with me and I find that I am not paying attention to them or don't care what they have to say, my relational circuits are off and I need to do something to get them back online. The best way to do this is to look away, find some curiosity and something to appreciate about them, then make eye contact and continue the conversation.

This ability to remain relational really shines when there are problems to solve. Mature people keep relationships bigger than problems. Immature people routinely sabotage relationships over even small challenges.

Habit 2: Act Like Yourself

Your true self is your relational self. When you stop acting like yourself, it is usually because you have gone into problem-solving mode. In their book *Escaping Enemy Mode*, Dr. Jim Wilder and retired general Ray Woolridge refer to a person who is stuck in the problem-solving part of their brain as living in enemy mode.[3] When I am in enemy mode, my focus is on winning, not on relating. When I go into enemy mode, I stop acting like myself and turn into someone else.

The ability to act like ourselves grows directly out of the fact that our joy center is also our identity center. We want this part of our brain in command—especially when we have to regulate upsetting emotions and navigate difficult situations. Losing access to this part of the brain means we lose the ability to act like ourselves.

Habit 3: Return to Joy

Remaining relational and acting like ourselves are the core habits of maturity. But now and then, all of us reach the end of our capacity and get overwhelmed. When this happens, we need to find ways to return to joy. To return to joy is to regain access to our joy center after our relational circuits have shut down. To develop this skill, we need to practice a tool called VCR—validate, comfort, recover.

Validate. I validate an emotion by correctly identifying what the emotion is and how big it is. I don't have to agree that the emotion is appropriate. I just have to recognize that this is, in fact, how I (or someone else) am feeling. For example, when I get upset with my wife, I may not be justified in my anger, but I have to admit that anger is, in fact, the emotion I feel. Correctly identifying the name of the emotion and how big it is validates the emotion. We can do this for ourselves when we struggle with our negative feelings. We can also do this with other people when they are struggling with their emotions.

The VCR process is a core parenting tool.[4] If my child falls and skins his knee and comes to me for comfort, it is important that I lead with validation. I might bend down and meet him at eye level and let my face reflect the emotion I see he is feeling. (This is nonverbal validation—connecting with him in his emotion just through body language.) If the child is crying, I stick out my bottom lip and show a sad face as if to say, "I see that you are sad and in pain." The goal is to get the child nodding his head in agreement that we have accurately seen how he feels.

Comfort. Comforting has to do with making problems smaller and more manageable. There are three basic strategies for doing this:

1. Tell the person (or yourself) what won't happen. This lets them know that the worst outcomes they may fear are not going to happen.
2. Offer a new perspective. Sometimes we make problems more manageable by changing the angle from which we are looking at the problem.
3. Make a simple plan. A simple plan has one or two steps that are going to move someone in a positive direction.

Thinking about the child who skinned his knee, after I validate his emotion (which might only take a few seconds), I can offer comfort by saying what won't happen, like, "Don't worry. It doesn't look that bad. We aren't going to have to do anything hard here." Then offering a new perspective, "A bloody knee is almost a badge of honor for a kid. Once you get through this, you'll have a scar there for a few days, letting the other kids know you can handle pain. You are a tough little guy." Of course, I also want to wash the wound, and apply some medicine and a Band-Aid.

It is important to remember that validation must always come before comforting. If we try to comfort someone before we validate their emotions, they will feel like we don't really care. Our attempts to comfort them will leave them feeling like a problem that needs to be solved, rather than a person needing love. We also need to do this for ourselves. If we skip validating ourselves and go straight to problem-solving, we end up minimizing our emotions.

Recovering. Recovering and returning to joy are basically the same thing. A person has recovered when their relational circuits reengage and their joy center is back in charge.

Once I have validated and comforted my little boy, I may ask, "Do you feel like going back outside and playing?" Or, "What do you feel like doing now?" By staying relationally engaged with kids as they recover, it is not uncommon for them to want to run back outside and play. They may also need just a bit more time to feel completely like themselves again, so a snack or a quieter game indoors might bridge the gap and help them fully recover.

This illustration focuses on helping children because that is where our kids learn these skills, but the same process applies to adults. Taking a few minutes to validate an emotion before trying to fix things goes a long way to helping people feel seen and understood.

Habit 4: Endure Hardship Well

This habit doubles as the definition of maturity. As I said at the beginning, mature people suffer well. This means that when they go through hard situations and difficult emotions they remain relational, act like themselves, return to joy quickly, and help those around them return to joy from whatever has them stuck. From this perspective, you can think of these RARE habits as a simple math equation:

Remaining relational

+

Acting like yourself

+

Returning to joy

=

Enduring hardship well

In building a factory for developing maturity, it is important to understand the product you are trying to create. It can also be helpful to recognize some of the signs that the product is defective.

THE FOUR A'S OF IMMATURITY

If you are looking for a quick diagnostic tool to help you recognize if someone is stuck at infant- or child-level maturity, you can use the four A's: anger, anxiety, avoidance, and addiction.

Anger

Because immature people have a small window of tolerance and low levels of emotional capacity, they tend to have a short fuse when it comes to their temper. They either bury their emotions until they explode or they fly into a rage at the drop of a hat. Both are signs of underdeveloped maturity.

Anxiety

Anxiety is anchored in imagination. When I live with low-emotional capacity, I learn to stay on guard for anything that might be emotionally overwhelming. As a result, my brain learns to look for things to fear.

Avoidance

When we lack the capacity to face difficult emotions, we naturally order our lives to avoid feeling those emotions. A classic example of an avoidant lifestyle is one where I work all day, then watch TV or play video games all evening. The problem with avoidance is that our lives get smaller with every emotion we avoid.

Addiction

Addiction is both a way to help us avoid unwanted emotions and to soothe ourselves from those emotions. Most addictions develop because they work. They temporarily help us avoid something we don't want to feel. However, the nature of addiction is that it takes more and more of the substance or experience to reach the same level of buzz. It takes more alcohol, more sexual stimulation, more adrenaline, and more of whatever it is we rely on to relieve our distress.

When it comes to addiction, two statements I have heard from Dr. Jim Wilder come to mind:

1. Addiction is the result of a catastrophic failure to attain maturity.[5] When we get stuck at infant- or child-level maturity, we will always be addicted to something. It is just a question of what our addiction will be. This is one of the main reasons that people often simply rotate addictions. They stop drinking alcohol but start bingeing TV. They quit smoking but start overeating. Until they repair the holes in their maturity development, they will never really become addiction free.

2. **The only thing anyone really fears is an emotion they can't handle.**[6] I had to stop and think about this one. But the more I thought about it, the more sense it made to me. I tend to think that I am afraid of pain. But the truth is that women often face great physical pain in childbirth only to choose to have another child. Both men and women often go through the pain of working out but enjoy the results so much and the community with others who workout that they happily endure the pain again. It is not really the pain we fear. It is the emotions pain evokes that overwhelm us.

As we think about building a maturity factory, not only does it help to know what a quality product looks like and the common defects that can occur, but it also helps to understand how healthy maturity development occurs.

THE STAGES OF MATURITY

According to *The Life Model*, there are five stages of maturity development between birth and death.[7] The first is infancy, which begins at birth and continues until weaning. The second is childhood, which begins at weaning and runs through puberty. The third stage is adulthood. This stage begins at puberty and continues until the birth of our first child. When we cross this significant divide, we leave the adult stage and become parents. We remain in the parent stage of life until our youngest child becomes an adult. At that point, we become elders.

Passing from one stage to another requires a type of death and resurrection. We die to life in the womb in order to live in a world where we breathe on our own. When we become children, we die to a life of having someone else take care of everything we need and begin to learn how to take care of ourselves. When we hit puberty, our bodies and brains go through a major transition, at which point we die to simply taking care of ourselves and become an adult who learns to take care of two people at the same time.[8]

By the time I marry and start a family of my own, I should have had several years of experience in being an adult. When my first child is born, I die to the relative simplicity of being an adult in an adult world and become a parent who now sacrificially meets my child's needs and begins to provide what they need to reach full maturity for their age.

When my youngest child becomes an adult, I go through another kind of death. I die to the role of serving as the primary caretaker of my children. I am now free to give my attention to the broader community. Having navigated the ups and downs of the various stages of life, I am primed to help others on that journey. I add wisdom and emotional stability to the groups I am in. A true elder excels at helping people deal with hard things without losing their joy.

You may notice that these five stages do not include adolescence. In most cultures throughout history, there was no category called "teenager" or "adolescent." In many ways, it is an artificial construct that creates something like a second childhood for people.

To better understand how we develop emotional maturity, let's look at a simple overview of the five developmental stages from birth to death.

Stage 1: Infant

At the infant stage, we are completely dependent on other people to recognize what we need and take care of us. Babies are good at letting people know when they are upset, but it is the adult's job to interpret the various whimpers, whining, screams, tears, and facial expressions. Someone has to notice what is happening and take care of the infant. They cannot take care of themselves.

When someone in an adult body is stuck at infant-level maturity, they still have trouble taking care of themselves. This is especially true of their emotions. They know how to express what they are feeling, but they do not know how to regulate their own emotions or recover from them. As a result, they are dependent on other people to recognize what they need and take care of them.

Stage 2: Child

The child stage of life is for learning how to take care of ourselves. We learn to potty, to dress ourselves, feed ourselves, make our beds, and do all of the tasks necessary to survive in this world. With help from others, we learn to ask for what we need and take responsibility for ourselves. If all goes well, children will start getting bored with this stage of life and be ready and excited to move into the adult years by the time puberty starts.

While it is obvious that children need to learn basic self-care when it comes to eating and dressing and so forth, it may not be as obvious that they also need to learn how to take care of themselves emotionally. There are two core problems that complicate maturity development for children.

1. Overprotection. *Helicopter parenting* often leads to underdeveloped emotional regulation skills. As a result, children don't learn how to recover from hard things. The term helicopter parent refers to a mom or dad who constantly hovers around a child to make sure they never feel pain or have to do anything difficult. These parents think they are taking good care of their children, but in reality they are sabotaging their emotional development. This type of parenting style can even extend into adulthood with the result that we actually interfere in the ability of our adult children to mature.[9]

In our book *Building Bounce*, Stefanie Hinman describes being tempted to keep her daughter from pain at school. She wanted to "bubble wrap" her little girl so that nothing bad ever happened to her. However, in praying about this, God prompted her that just as children needed to develop a healthy immune system to repel infection, so they needed to develop a healthy emotional system that could handle all sorts of emotions and recover. She learned that it was not her job, as a mom, to keep her daughter from having to feel certain emotions. It was her job to provide a safe, secure place for recovering from those emotions.[10]

When kids know they can face hard situations and still be okay, life becomes an adventure. If they can face big emotions and do hard tasks without losing their joy, the world gets bigger. In contrast, the more emotions they fear, the smaller their world gets. If they fear shame and have to avoid anything that makes them feel shame, their world shrinks just a little bit. If they fear anger, and have to avoid anything that exposes them to anger, their world shrinks some more. Without the emotional capacity to face their fears and recover, they will craft an avoidant lifestyle filled with addiction.

2. Under-Protection. The opposite of helicopter parents who bubble wrap their kids are parents who are so preoccupied with their own problems they neglect their children and force them to parent themselves. In many cases, the child has to fill the role of parent in the family or even the parents themselves. These "parentified children" learn that if they don't step up and take care of the family, no one else will.

Kids who are left to parent themselves often develop *upside-down maturity*. They look very mature on the outside. They tend to be very responsible and are good at making sure everyone is taken care of, but they never learn how to care for themselves.

Both overprotection and under-protection produce kids with low emotional capacity.

Trauma stunts maturity development. An ideal maturity development process is one in which children are raised not only by parents with a high level of maturity, but by their extended family (including mature aunts, uncles, and grandparents) with extensive input from other members of the community who are functioning at adult-, parent-, and elder-level maturity. When children are getting this much input from people who have attained advanced levels of maturity, their own maturity development happens almost automatically.

Trauma interrupts this ideal. In fact, anything that interrupts this process can be termed *trauma* because it will stunt a child's maturity development, and stunted maturity can lead to catastrophic emotional and behavioral problems.

According to *The Life Model*, there are two primary types of trauma that can interrupt maturity development. The first is B trauma. "B" stands for "bad" and refers to the bad stuff that happens to us. This is what we typically think of as trauma and includes abuse of all kinds. The second type is A trauma. "A" stands for "absence" and refers to the absence of the good stuff we need like an intact family, nurture, training, and lots of adults modeling adult behavior.[11]

In some ways, B trauma is easier to resolve than A trauma. Dealing with B trauma generally requires the Holy Spirit's healing of past memories, removing demonic influences through spiritual warfare, and replacing false beliefs with true beliefs. Overcoming A Trauma takes more time because it involves learning skills and habits that got missed. If someone grew up with an absent father and an alcoholic mother, they are going to need to do more than forgive both their mom and dad for abandoning them in different ways. They will have to deal with both the A trauma of what they missed and the B trauma of the bad things that happened. They will need to repair the damage done by the B trauma through strategies that promote healing and freedom. But they will also need to grow resilience as they repair the damage done by the A trauma. This will take extended relational work because both their joy center and joy pathways will be underdeveloped. Mastering the skills needed to regulate their emotions and live with relational joy can take longer than the healing itself.

Learning new skills later in life is sort of like trying to learn a new language as an adult. If we want to learn a new language later in life, it is going to take a lot more intentional effort on our part than if we had learned it when we were young. The same is true of the relational and emotional skills we miss. Developing them later in life is going to be harder and take some focused work.

Understanding A and B trauma can help make sense out of the statement that everyone has a wounded heart. I have spoken to several people who claim they have never been wounded. They often come from good families and never experienced anything we would call "abuse." Many of them have no major B trauma in their lives. However, in most cases, when I explain A trauma, their eyes light up with recognition. It is possible to have good parents who have gaps in their maturity that lead to holes in their parenting. In addition to explaining how the absence of good things can stunt our development, I will often note that B trauma doesn't have to be dramatic in order to have a big impact. Here is an example of what I mean.

When I was twelve, I was one of the best baseball players on my Little League team. I hoped to be named the "Most Valuable Player" of the league. One day, we had an important game, and I had a chance to score the winning run. However, I got called out sliding into third base. In the heat of the moment, I was livid. I was sure I was safe and that the umpire had made a bad call. I was also ashamed, because it was common knowledge that you never get thrown out at third in a close game. As I left the field, I was crying and angry. When I got to the car, my dad—who was normally the model of emotional empathy—said, "Is this any way for someone who wants to be the MVP to act?" The comment stabbed me like a knife. I needed someone to validate my emotions and help me recover. Instead, I got more shame. It wounded my heart.

Years later, I realized that I routinely avoided putting myself in a position to feel shame. I didn't want to do things unless I was confident I would succeed. While processing this realization, the Lord reminded me of this memory. It wasn't a huge trauma. My dad had not been abusive. On a scale of one to ten of the pain that people experience, it was not a very big trauma. But the lie it taught me was huge. As a result of that tiny wound, I believed the lie that I was not allowed to make mistakes. I believed I had to be perfect. Agreeing to that lie led to a vow that I would never put myself in a position to feel that kind of shame again. The result was a stronghold that created an area of bondage in my life. I don't tell this story to paint my dad in a bad light. I tell this story to illustrate how even a small wound can have a profound impact on the way we live.

Thinking about the two women mentioned at the beginning of the chapter, they both had A and B trauma in their lives. The second woman simply had a lot more of both. As a result, her journey was going to be much more complicated because there was a lot more repair needed. For her, breakthrough was going to require not only freedom from a few habits. It was going to require developing a level of maturity she had not attained to at that point. This was going to take more than a few prayer sessions and some good advice. There were skills she needed to develop that could only be learned with extensive relational interaction with a lot of people. She needed more than individual counseling. She needed a spiritual family.

Stage 3: Adult

Adult-level maturity must be earned. We have to master all of the skills needed to care for ourselves so that we can enter a world of adults and hold our own. Skills we miss learning as children leave holes in our maturity as adults. These holes are often related to specific emotions that push us beyond our window of tolerance.

Earlier in this chapter, I referenced the four RARE habits that characterize adult-level maturity: remaining relational, acting like ourselves, returning to joy, and enduring hardship well. The first two habits stress the idea that adults have a large window of tolerance, which allows them to remain relational and act like themselves despite big emotions. The third habit—returning to joy—refers to the ability to recover quickly when we do get pushed beyond our window of tolerance. When you put them all together, you get someone who is able to live with adult-level maturity.

Stage 4: Parent

While adults are good at win-win scenarios that allow them to care for themselves and have something left to share with others, parents are ready to sacrificially provide for infants and guide children to become adults by the time they reach puberty. People with parent-level maturity take the lead in turning their home into a maturity-producing factory. In fact, parenting is one of the most leadership-intensive activities we ever undertake. It is our job to create engagement in what matters and train our kids to avoid what is harmful and excel in what gives life.

Ideally, people in ministry—especially pastors, missionaries, prayer ministers, and counselors—have attained parent- or elder-level maturity. This means they can return to joy from all of the SADSAD emotions themselves and guide others to do the same. One cause of burnout among people helpers is the stress that comes from trying to fill the role of spiritual parent or elder while still an emotional child.

Stage 5: Elder

An elder is someone whose youngest child has reached adult-level maturity. These people are often empty nesters whose kids are raising families of their own. Through years of navigating the challenges of adult- and parent-level challenges, elders have earned a level of maturity that makes them highly stable, full of joy, and able to bring wisdom to the problems of the community.

Elders often function as surrogate parents for people who were not fully parented. In this way, they extend their family and help people fill the holes in their maturity development that enable them to develop the skills and habits they missed along the way.

EMOTIONAL WEIGHTLIFTING

When I think of what it takes to build the emotional capacity to live within my window of tolerance, I usually think of weightlifting. When I go to the gym, my choices are limited by my capacity. It has been a long time since I have lifted any significant weight. There was a time when I could work out with over two hundred pounds on the bar. Today, I don't think I could lift that even once. But what I could do is start to grow my capacity. If I started an intentional workout program, in a few months, I could likely lift that much weight. It is the same with emotional capacity.

Our capacity limits the choices that are available to us. Thus, we need to grow our capacity to handle emotional weight in the same way that we might need to grow our capacity to handle physical weight.

When it comes to building muscle, the growth in my muscles does not happen while I am at the gym and lifting weights. It happens while I am resting and letting my muscles repair. The pain you feel after weight-lifting is a sign that your muscles are repairing themselves from the damage done during the workout. But it is also a sign that your muscles are growing. There is a reason weightlifters say, "No pain, no gain." Some even say they learn to like the pain, because it means their muscles are growing and they are achieving their goals.

HOW WE BUILD MATURITY

There are three key elements needed in maturity development: joy workouts, bounce workouts, and trauma repair.

Joy Workouts

In order for us to grow our emotional capacity we need to do regular *joy workouts*. A joy workout has two parts to it. The first part is about sharing joy with another person in a way that floods our brains with joy-producing chemicals like dopamine and endorphins. When babies are first born, their primary form of bonding is smell and touch. They recognize mommy's smell and touch, and those help to create a safe, secure attachment for the infant. A few months into their development, babies begin to attach primarily through eye contact. They search for eyes that are happy to see them. Sharing joy smiles happens when we make eye contact with a little one in a way that communicates, "I think you are wonderful, and I am happy to be with you!" Babies can literally start bouncing with joy and overflow with giggling just from happy-to-see-you eye contact.

The second part of a joy workout is rest. You may notice that a baby can go from total ecstasy at all the attention she is getting to suddenly looking away as if something is wrong. This is perfectly normal. It means the joy center in the baby's brain has reached capacity, and she needs to rest. If you give her a break she will recover in a few minutes and once again look for eye contact to see if you are still happy to see her.

These joy workouts grow the joy center in the brain the way working out with weights grows our muscles. There is no way to build emotional capacity without the joy workouts needed to grow our joy centers. There are two issues it can help to understand related to joy workouts.

1. Rest is important. Some people do not understand why babies look away when it feels like they are having so much fun. Instead of allowing them to rest, they try to keep them engaged and giggling. This may seem like a good idea, but it is not. It is similar to tickling someone too long. It stops being fun and becomes traumatic. If infants are not allowed to rest on their own schedule and don't get the breaks they need, they will not feel safe. Instead of giving them a joy workout, it can turn into a fear workout. If babies learn that joy can end up in pain, they may look for joy less often, and the roots are laid for developing fear bonds.

2. We never outgrow our need for joy workouts. As children get older they still need a rhythm of happy-to-see-you joy and happy-to-be-with-you rest. When we take our toddlers to the park to play, they often want mommy and daddy with them everywhere they go. They need the security of lots of attachment as they try new things. You may notice that just a little bit of play in a new environment can make toddlers sleepy. It maxes out their capacity. As our little ones get used to the park and it stops being unfamiliar, they will not want us around as much. In a sense, we are like the joy gas station for them. They come and see us whenever they need some joy fuel or maybe some relational rest time, then they go right back to playing. For insecure parents, or for parents who do not understand what is happening, the growing independence of the child can feel like rejection. But they are actually right on schedule for developing the emotional capacity they need to deal with the adventure of playing at the park.

We are able to grow our capacity for joy and peace for as long as we live (unless brain damage or something similar gets in the way). In our book *The 4 Habits of Joy-Filled Marriages*, my coauthor Chris Coursey tells the story of how he and his wife started doing appreciation exercises before they went to bed. One of their favorites was called 3-3-3. Each of them shared three things they appreciated about the past day, three things they appreciated about each other with an example of when they had seen it, and three things they appreciated about God. Chris said the exercise helped them quiet their minds, and it was not uncommon for them both to fall asleep within ten minutes of their fifteen-minute joy workout.[12]

Bounce Workouts

Growing our ability to recover from upsetting emotions can be thought of as building bounce.[13] Just as joy workouts help us grow our capacity for joy, *bounce workouts* help us build our capacity to recover from upsetting emotions and return to joy.

Bounce workouts are based on vulnerability and empathy. Vulnerability allows people to see what we are really thinking and feeling. Empathy is when they meet us where we are at before trying to fix us or help us recover. Most of us learn through experience that it is not safe to be completely vulnerable with some people. We have discovered that people will use our weakness against us, and we have found that the world can be predatory. Other kids may laugh at our emotions or mock our failings. Parents may dismiss our emotions as silly or overly dramatic. They may also punish us for our emotions or openly shame us for letting them be known.

Building bounce and learning how to return to joy are the same thing. So, in the same way that VCR (validate, comfort, recover) is essential to returning to joy, it is also essential to a good bounce workout. Kids make a lot of mistakes and feel a lot of emotions, so parents get lots of opportunities for bounce workouts. We attune to our child's emotional state, validate their emotions, comfort them relationally, and help them recover. The more this happens, the more emotional stability the child develops.

If we are older and we are trying to build our ability to bounce back from upsetting emotions, it can help to practice VCR on ourselves. It can also help to tell joy stories about times we experienced upsetting emotions but bounced back. A joy story is not a story about a time we were happy. It is a story about a time we experienced something emotional and either recovered or acted like ourselves.

Stories help us integrate the two sides of our brains. They utilize the attachments systems on the right side of the brain and the narrative systems on the left side of the brain. Bringing these together helps us experience a whole brain and reinforces to us how it is like us to act when we go through hard things.

Joy stories follow a simple pattern: STEP.

Setting: Where was I when the situation happened that caused the big emotion?

Trigger: What was the event that triggered my emotion?

Emotion: Practice validation here. Accurately name the emotion and how big it was.

Point: What is the point of the story? It should teach a lesson either about how I acted like myself, returned to joy, or wish I had responded.[14]

What we don't want are stories that follow a pattern that reinforce why we are stuck. For example, I don't want to say, "This bad thing happened when I was in high school. It made me feel this bad emotion. And that is why I am so messed up today." That is not a joy story. Instead, I might say:

Setting: "I played basketball in college, and our team went out of town for one of our games."

Trigger: "After the game was over, I headed back to the van we were using and heard crying. I was the first one there and noticed the sobbing was coming from a girl who volunteered as a manager. This girl was overweight and I knew she had faced a lot of pain in her life."

Emotion: "I felt afraid because this seemed like a problem that was too big for me to handle. I could feel my heart race because I didn't know what to do. Part of me wanted to pretend I didn't notice and let someone else handle it, but I realized it wasn't like me to do that." **Point:** "I acted like myself by asking her what was wrong and listening to her story. Partly because of her weight, she felt rejected by everyone and someone at the game had made a mean remark about how heavy she was. She told me she was tired of trying to pretend she was happy. I wasn't sure what to do, so I just stayed present and let her talk. By the time two more people came by, she thanked me for listening. All I had really done was to not abandon her, but by acting like myself, I was able to make a big problem smaller."

TRAUMA REPAIR

Even when we build our capacity for joy and our capacity to return to joy, unresolved trauma from the past can cause us to "leak" joy in a way that makes it hard to grow. The most effective trauma repair strategies I have found are listening prayer and defeating demons. While strategies like joy workouts and bounce workouts are effective solutions to A trauma, listening prayer and deliverance are effective for resolving B trauma.

Collectively, all five strategies related to the five engines that drive our emotions play a role in helping us repair damage caused by trauma and grow our capacity to live with joy. When we combine the five strategies with the five stages of maturity development, they form a matrix that helps us understand the kind of intervention that may be needed depending on the engine affected and the maturity level of the person involved.

	BODY	BELIEFS	BONDS	SPIRIT	DEMONS
INFANT Watching	Infants experience security when their needs are met without needing to behave a certain way.	Infants do not develop core beliefs. Instead, they watch and "download" what they see.	Infants form joy bonds when they get regular joy workouts. They form fear bonds when they miss out on these workouts or are forced to bond to scary people.	Infants watch as others pray and listen to God on their behalf.	Infants watch as others deal with warfare issues on their behalf.
CHILD Learning	People at child-level maturity can take care of their own physical needs, but may not help you take care of yours.	People at child-level maturity can learn to "feed themselves" from Scripture with help.	People stuck at child-level maturity are prone to fear mapping their world because of a lack of safe, secure attachments.	People at child-level maturity need to be taught how to pray. Model prayers can be helpful.	People at child-level maturity can learn to recognize and remove demonic activity for themselves.
ADULT Practicing	Adults consider what is best for their group's health while taking care of themselves.	Adults are able to understand what they believe and why they believe it.	Adults create belonging wherever they go.	Adults need a strong group to fuel their spiritual growth.	Adults help defend their group from spiritual attack.
PARENT Training	Parents manage diet, sleep, exercise, and medical care for infants and children.	Parents lead children in developing a worldview and values that reflect the family and the Bible.	Parents create belonging in a family. They pass on relational skills by modeling and instructing.	Parents model and train children in spiritual disciplines and relational joy.	Parents pray against the enemy and train their children in warfare basics.
ELDER Blessing	Elders keep their bodies healthy. They also look after the general health of their community.	Elders serve as a source of wisdom about the worldview and values of the culture.	Elders create belonging within a community. They care for those without families.	Elders live in the Spirit and spend extended time in prayer for their communities.	Elders defend their communities from spiritual attack and handle the most difficult warfare cases.

Now that we have spent a few chapters exploring maturity, it is time to take a deeper dive into the five strategies that help us BUILD maturity. In the next chapter, we will explore the first strategy—Be Aware of Your Body.

CHAPTER 6

BE AWARE OF
YOUR BODY

IN HIS BOOK *Could It Be This Simple?*, psychiatrist Timothy R. Jennings tells the story of a Bible teacher who came from a tradition that did not believe in medication.[1] The man developed a debilitating disorder that gradually took away his ability to function. No matter how much time he spent meditating on Scripture and praying for relief, his condition simply got worse. However, he resolutely refused medication and eventually found himself in a padded cell completely unable to manage his emotions.

Dr. Jennings was called in and finally convinced the man to try the appropriate medication for his condition. Within a few days, he showed significant improvement. Within a few months, he was able to return to his position as a Bible instructor.

Stories like these remind us that sometimes our emotional conditions are being driven by problems in the body. When this is the case, the only solution that will help is one that addresses this engine. Thus, Strategy #1 for finding breakthrough is to be aware of our bodies.

For those of us who are biblical counselors and prayer ministers, we can sometimes forget how significant the body can be in driving the way people feel. We all know that something as simple as lack of sleep can impact our emotions, so it is important to encourage people to be aware of the role the body can play in driving our emotions and direct them to the proper help.

BRAIN INJURIES AND OUR EMOTIONS

Years ago, I watched the movie *Regarding Henry* starring Harrison Ford. It is about a high-powered lawyer whose brain was damaged by a gunshot during a robbery. The wound damaged the part of his brain that helped him remember who he was and how it was like him to act. Throughout the movie, we learn that he had not been a very good person. He was cheating on his wife, lying at his job, and—prior to the gunshot wound—lived as a classic narcissist. The injury to his brain turned out to be a blessing because it gave him a second chance to decide what sort of person he wanted to be.

Prior to watching that movie, I don't think I had thought much about the role of the brain in our emotions beyond its role in our beliefs. Later, I saw a TED talk by popular psychiatrist Daniel Amen, in which he claimed that mild, traumatic brain injury was a major cause of psychiatric illness.[2] It makes sense that brain injuries can affect our brain's ability to regulate emotions.

In this talk, he showed a scan taken of a fifteen-year-old boy's damaged brain. This boy had fallen when he was three years old and had been knocked unconscious for only a few minutes. It seemed like a minor event, but the untreated damage had catastrophic consequences for his life.

The teenager often had random violent outbursts. For the past several years, he had been medicated, taken through behavior modification treatment, cognitive therapy, and—when Dr. Amen met him—had just been kicked out of a residential treatment program for the third time.

Once Dr. Amen got involved, he took a scan of the boy's brain. It revealed significant damage that was clearly responsible for the inability to regulate his emotions. Once the brain injury was recognized and a brain rehabilitation program was initiated, this boy's symptoms resolved.

According to Dr. Amen, undiagnosed brain injuries like the one in this story are "a major cause of homelessness, drug and alcohol abuse, depression, panic attacks, ADHD, and suicide."[3]

In my opening illustration, I cited the positive impact that medication can have on our emotions. However, there can be danger in medication as well. Dr. Amen is a psychiatrist who routinely prescribes medications, but he offered this warning:

> Before imaging, I always felt like I was throwing darts in the dark at my patients and had hurt some of them, which horrified me. There is a reason that most psychiatric medications have black box warnings. Give them to the wrong person, and you can precipitate a disaster.[4]

As a minister, I am not in a position to diagnose and treat the body. The point here is that we need to be aware of the body and make sure competent people are looking into the problems that can arise from it.

SCHIZOPHRENIA

A classic example of a physical condition that can drive the way we live is schizophrenia. As someone who has done a lot of spiritual warfare ministry, I often get asked if schizophrenia is demonic. The answer is emphatically no. Schizophrenia is a physical problem that does not resolve by evicting demons.

However, this does not mean that people who suffer with schizophrenia cannot have demons. As we have already noted, demons are like sharks. When they see blood in the water, they don't say, "This person is in enough trouble. I'll stay out of it." I spoke with one psychiatrist who has extensive experience working with schizophrenia, and he said it was not uncommon for his clients to have two sets of voices. One tended to be characterized by random, often disconnected thoughts. The other was darker and often more religious. The psychiatrist had learned to ask his clients if they had a darker set of voices they didn't like to mention. Many of them looked at him with surprise and said something like, "Who told you about those?"

In our secular society, people may get misdiagnosed with schizophrenia because it is the most common category secular practitioners have for people who hear voices. I have worked with more than one person who had been diagnosed with schizophrenia but had their symptoms completely resolve when they got rid of the demons that plagued them. One of the first people I met like this was a woman who had been clinically diagnosed with schizophrenia. The diagnosis made sense. The radio would talk to her with special messages just for her. People on TV often spoke directly to her. She had voices in her head telling her to hurt people. I never challenged her diagnosis or suggested she get off her meds. That is not my job. Instead, we explored her life story to see if there were experiences that might have opened doors to the demonic. It turned out there were a lot.

Ancestrally, her family were pagans who worshiped false gods, and that practice had never been renounced. She had participated in almost every kind of occult practice I knew to ask about. In addition, she had lived with her boyfriend in sexual immorality for over a year. To make things worse, when she broke up with him, he put a curse on her. It turns out he was a warlock. So, even though this young lady was a professing Christian, she had opened a lot of doors for demonic activity in her life.

We spent two sessions dealing with these spiritual warfare issues. By the time we were done, she wasn't hearing voices anymore and the TV wasn't talking to her. She no longer had any compulsions toward violence. In her case, she had been misdiagnosed.

BASIC HEALTH AND GOOD HABITS

Several years ago, I read a magazine story about an overweight man who became so depressed that he wanted to kill himself.[5] However, he also wanted to take care of his family and knew that his insurance policy would not pay them if he committed suicide. So, he settled on a unique plan. Realizing he was in terrible physical health, he decided to run several miles, expecting to die of a heart attack.

He put his affairs in order and went running. He pushed himself so hard he passed out. When he woke up and realized he wasn't dead, he decided to try again the next day. Once again, he ran until he passed out, but he didn't die. So, he decided to try again. You can probably see where this is going. Slowly he discovered that he was starting to look forward to his daily run. As he lost weight and got in better shape, he started to feel better. Soon, he joined a running club and made some new friends. Within a few months, his life had turned around and his depression was gone.

This story made an impression on me because it touches on all three of the physical engines. This man got his body in shape. His beliefs changed, and he formed joy bonds with some peers. It is also a great reminder that sometimes just taking good care of our bodies can make a profound difference in how we feel. It is not uncommon for diet, exercise, and sleep to have a major impact on our emotions.

"THE BODY KEEPS THE SCORE"

Dr. Bessel van der Kolk is the former president of the International Society for Traumatic Stress Studies and the author of the bestselling book *The Body Keeps the Score*. While we all know that our bodies can impact our emotions, his book highlights the fact that our emotions can have a major impact on our bodies as well.[6]

According to Dr. van der Kolk, "We all have jobs and situations that are really unpleasant. But the moment that a situation is over, it is over.

The problem with trauma is that when it's over, your body continues to relive it."[7]

A physician once told me he thought that as much as 80 percent of what he saw in patients was "psychosomatic." I used to think that meant people believed they had problems and so they developed problems. But I think he was saying the same thing as Dr. van der Kolk. He was recognizing that most of what was wrong in the bodies of the people he treated had emotional trauma at its root.

If our bodies are like cars, then low-energy emotions are like stepping on the brakes and high-energy emotions are like stepping on the accelerator. When we have both low-energy emotions (like shame, sadness, disgust, and despair) and high-energy emotions (like anger and fear) that are happening at the same time, it is a bit like holding down the brakes and the accelerator at the same time. It can literally make our bodies shake. You can easily see the kind of damage to the body long-term stress can have.

In order to help people de-stress their bodies, yoga has become a very common prescription for traumatized people. In *The Body Keeps the Score*, Dr. van der Kolk spends quite a bit of time promoting yoga as an almost essential part of trauma recovery. There is, of course, a problem with this—especially for Christians—and that is the fact that yoga is a Hindu religious practice. Its purpose is not to de-stress the body but to commune with Hindu deities.

A former practitioner who studied under a Hindu guru writes:

> The true purpose of yoga is enlightenment. The word "yoga" means "yoked"—and those who believe in it, insist it means being yoked with Universal Consciousness. This "enlightened" state supposedly happens when the kundalini power rises through the spine, activating and aligning something adherents call "the chakras" (seven energy discs in the body).[8]

I have met with more than one person who had a "kundalini" spirit from doing kundalini yoga. One of them temporarily lost the ability to speak and began sticking out his tongue like a snake and rocking back and forth in snake-like movements. Kundalini is routinely depicted as a serpent coiled up at the base of the spine. The purpose of yoga is to release this serpent spirit and energize the chakras.[9]

Both secularists and Christians often try to separate the stretching and deep breathing exercises involved in yoga from the spiritual realities they are meant to invoke. However, several researchers have shown that the positions themselves are meant to depict submission to a particular Hindu deity.

My point in all of this is that Christians should find an alternative to yoga. I know there are "holy yoga" clubs in churches that listen to Christian music and meditate on biblical thoughts, but honestly, using a sequence of positions rooted in Hindu religious practices still makes me wonder if it is wise. There are enough red flags to suggest we avoid the potential open doors involved in this practice. Quieting your mind and de-stressing your body are good goals. Developing flexibility is a fine ambition. We just need to find ways to do these things that are not devoted to pagan deities.

QUIETING

Quieting is the practice of calming racing thoughts and relaxing a stressed body. According to Raymond Jones and Jim Wilder, quieting is the number one predictor of stable emotional health.[10] People who are able to quiet from upsetting emotions easily have a major advantage over people who cannot do this. Without the ability to quiet, we will find ourselves trapped in a body that is being run by stressful emotions.

When I first learned about quieting, I was suspicious. It sounded like a New Age practice. But the New Age practice is about emptying your mind for the purpose of communing with a spiritual reality other than the true God. There is a difference between emptying your mind for the purpose of opening it to a spiritual experience and quieting your mind. A quiet mind is simply a mind at peace.

In Psalm 131:2, David writes, "Instead, I have calmed and quieted my soul like a weaned child with its mother; my soul is like a weaned child" (CSB). This is a beautiful description of quieting. You have likely seen a baby dozing in contented bliss after being fed. The child isn't sleeping deeply, but is at perfect peace. This verse occurs in one of the shortest chapters in the Bible. It consists of only three verses. In the first verse David writes, "I do not get involved with things too great or too wonderous for me" (Ps. 131:1 CSB). This speaks to a quiet mind that is not fixated on all of the problems of the world. Then we read, "Instead, I have calmed and quieted my soul like a weaned child with its mother; my soul is like a weaned child" (Ps. 131:2 CSB). In the final verse, David urges Israel, saying, "Put your hope in [Yahweh] both now and forever" (Ps. 131:3 CSB). The image here paints a picture of Yahweh as the mother and David as the baby. He is at peace despite the big issues going on in the world because he is contentedly bonded to Yahweh.

BEST PRACTICES FOR QUIETING

It is important to learn how to quiet our bodies from the emotions that can take hold of them. This is true for a number of reasons: (1) it is bad for our physical health to allow stress to control our bodies, (2) it is miserable to endure the physical symptoms of emotions like anxiety, and (3) releasing stress from our bodies helps us recover from upsetting emotions.

Quieting our minds is different than quieting our bodies. We quiet our minds by replacing toxic thoughts with good thoughts. We quiet our bodies by calming our amygdala and changing our body chemistry. Here are four practices that can help you quiet your body when you feel stressed.[11] These practices can be remembered with the acronym BEST: breathe in a box, exaggerate emotions, soothe the senses, tense your muscles, and then relax them.

B—Breathe in a Box

In the military, this technique is routinely taught to help soldiers keep their emotions under control during high-stress situations. Being intentional about taking deep breaths and being in control of your breathing helps to regulate your emotions.

The specific skill of breathing in a box works like this. Inhale deeply while you count to four. Hold your breath while you count to four again. Exhale completely as you count to four in your mind. Wait for a count of four and repeat the process.

When teaching this process to children, Stefanie Hinman—a therapist and author of *Building Bounce with Kids*—has them blow on the soup and smell the soup.[12] Blowing on the soup requires exhaling and blowing all of the air out of your lungs. Smelling the soup means inhaling deeply and refilling your lungs with air.

E—Exaggerate Your Emotions

This may seem counterintuitive, but have you ever noticed that it doesn't usually help to tell someone to just calm down? It is actually easier to regulate our emotions if we exaggerate them first. Exaggerating our emotions helps us be more aware of them, which can make the rest of the quieting process more effective.

A good way to exaggerate your emotion is to overemphasize what your body does when you feel a particular emotion. You might stick out your bottom lip and pout to exaggerate sadness. You might throw your hands over your head and gasp while making your eyes big to exaggerate fear. You could flex your muscles, flare your nostrils, and grimace to exaggerate anger. Sometimes the process of exaggeration makes us laugh, which helps relieve the tension in and of itself.

S—Soothe Your Senses

It is often helpful to do something to soothe tense muscles. Taking a hot bath, cuddling on a comfy chair with a weighted blanket, or creating a relaxing atmosphere can help us soothe our senses. As with exaggerating our emotions, it can sometimes help to do something shocking first and then soothing. For example, it can help reset your body chemistry to take a cold shower and then warm up by the fire. Splashing cold water on your face has a mild shocking effect that can make it easier to calm afterward.

T—Tense Your Muscles, Then Relax Them

Another way of taking control of your body is to intentionally tense and then relax various muscle groups in your body. You might tighten your thigh muscles for four seconds, then relax them, rub them lightly, then repeat. The process of increasing tension and then relaxing that tension is a theme in these practices.

A WORD ON THE NEW AGE MOVEMENT

I see the New Age movement as the syncretistic combining of pagan and occult practices with scientific explanations. Syncretism is the unnatural blending of worldviews and the practices that spring from those worldviews. The New Age focuses on spirituality and especially spirituality and the body. Because evangelical Christians have tended to focus on spirituality almost exclusively in terms of truth, we can be suspicious of any spirituality that includes the body. What I am trying to do here is build a strong wall between true Christianity and the New Age movement while taking seriously the idea that our physical bodies, our emotions, and our spirituality are connected. They are just not connected in the way the New Age movement teaches.

In the early church, the Gnostics represented another syncretistic movement that brought Eastern beliefs and practices into the church. What I am promoting here has nothing to do with either the New Age or Gnosticism. It is simply an attempt to fill a hole that has commonly been present among Bible-believing Christians, and that is to recognize the role of the body in our emotions and the help that is available by dealing with physical issues.

THE BODY MATTERS

The first essential strategy for breakthrough is to be aware of our bodies. This strategy is directly tied to the idea that our body is one of the five core engines that drive our emotions.

If you are looking for a breakthrough that has eluded you, it can help to do the basics first. Get enough sleep. Eat healthy. Exercise. But it may also be important to seek professional help. Whether it is a brain injury or a chemical imbalance, physical problems can be a major driver of negative emotions and compulsive behaviors.

In the next chapter, we will explore Strategy #2 for finding breakthrough—dealing with the battle for our mind and the engine of beliefs.

CHAPTER 7

UNLEASH YOUR
BELIEFS

WHEN I WAS YOUNG, I played a lot of sports. One day, my dad had me listen to some cassette tapes called "Psycho-Cybernetics" by Maxwell Maltz. A book by the same name written in 1960 has sold millions of copies. At the heart of what I took from these tapes is the idea that our imaginations are more powerful than our choices. I remember listening to a lot of stories about athletes who included focused imagination in their workouts.[1] They would picture themselves doing things perfectly. A wide receiver would spend thirty minutes sitting in a chair as he pictured himself catching every ball thrown to him. Golfers would close their eyes and imagine themselves playing a round of golf perfectly. One study mentioned on the tapes was about basketball players who were divided into two groups. One shot a hundred free throws each day, the other sat in a chair and pictured themselves making a hundred free throws each day. Both groups saw exactly the same level of improvement.

At the time, I was playing Little League. I started practicing the power of imagination when I pitched. Before every pitch I would take two seconds to imagine myself throwing a perfect pitch. I made the pitch in my head before I started my windup. In one of the first games I tried this, I struck out twelve batters in four innings. Sadly, because there was a limit to how many innings we could pitch in one week, I had to stop, but I was on my way to potentially tying the record for most strikeouts in a game.

The point here isn't that I was a bad pitcher who suddenly became a good pitcher. The point was that harnessing my imagination allowed me to pitch with a supreme amount of confidence—and we usually perform better when we are confident. Experiencing this at a young age made me a believer in the power of thoughts, ideas, beliefs, and mental images— and the importance of unleashing our beliefs.

My father often said, "People may not practice what they say they believe. But they always practice what they really believe." He understood that beliefs have a profound impact on how we feel and the choices we make.

He also understood that our emotions can't tell a true belief from a false one. Thus, I may say I trust God, but my actions say otherwise. I may say I believe the Bible, but still not trust God with specific problems in my life. Here are some classic examples of how beliefs can drive our emotions:

- A beautiful woman believes she is fat and becomes anorexic.
- A divorced man looks at his bank account, his credit card statements, and his lack of investments and imagines a catastrophic future, causing a panic attack over something that has not happened. His emotions are responding to what he can imagine happening.
- A young woman in her thirties wants to get married but sees no prospects on her horizon and becomes depressed believing her dream is impossible.
- A middle-aged executive sees a millennial walk into his office for an interview and feels disgust. He has formed opinions about millenials, and what he believes causes him to miss out on his company's next great leader.

I'm sure we all have stories of believing something that drove our emotions, only to see our emotions completely changed when we discovered there was another side to the story.

BELIEFS ABOUT GOD

One of the areas in which we experience the power of beliefs most often is in our walk with God. We often believe in good theology. We believe God is omniscient and omnipotent and omnipresent. But sometimes that just makes the problem worse. We question, *If God is all of those things, and if God comes through for some people, why hasn't He come through for me?* It is not uncommon for hurting people to believe that God is cruel or distant. Or to think, *If the problem isn't God, it must be me. If God is not cruel and distant, perhaps I am such a horrible person that God can't or won't help me.* It is all too common for people to ping pong back and forth between distrusting God and despising themselves.

Many Christians struggle with something William Backus called "the hidden rift with God."[2] In his book by that title, Backus suggests that Christians often deny the depth of their anger with God because they want to be "good Christians." So, instead of dealing with the pain and the beliefs they have formed because of that pain, they just try to work harder. They read their Bible more. They volunteer at church. They even go to counseling. But nothing seems to work. Nothing works because they are dealing with surface-level issues and surface-level beliefs. However, in the process, they have often not yet addressed the root issues of their bondage.

Years ago, I heard a chapel speaker say something that has stayed with me ever since. He was talking about beliefs and emotions and his talk went something like this:

My mother dies. Your mother dies. I go into a depression. You don't. Why is that? It is because what my mother dying means to me is different than what your mother dying means to you.

His point was that the meaning (beliefs) we attach to events determines the emotional impact they have on us. I agree with that, but can't help but notice that another reason for the different reactions in his illustration was the nature of the attachment represented in these relationships. I suspect one person had a joy bond with his mother and the other did not.

That having been said, attachment pain and fear bonds affect what we believe, and changing what we believe can have a major impact on our emotions.

POCKETS OF PAIN

I have a friend whose father had a split personality.[3] One part of him was a hardworking farmer and a deacon at his church. The other part of him was sadistic and perverted. When my friend was a little girl, her father trafficked her to men in his community. One of those men was her pastor. Talk about growing up with a twisted view of reality!

Today, this lady runs a ministry that helps people who have been trafficked or sexually abused. She understands that most of these women struggle to believe that God is good, just like she did. One of the lessons I have learned from her is that people often have pockets of pain in their hearts. These pockets of pain are home to deeply rooted lies about God. They also tend to believe lies about themselves and the world in which they live. When the emotions related to these pockets of pain get triggered, they can become totally different people with a totally different worldview. Part of them believes the truth, but part of them believes something completely untrue.

The idea of "pockets of pain" has helped me understand why I sometimes trust God implicitly and sometimes fail to trust in Him in very basic ways. I may trust Him to work all things together for good in one area of my life, but feel completely alone and unloved in another. It has helped me understand how it is possible to have such completely opposite reactions to life by understanding that pockets of pain keep me "double-minded" and, as we read in James 1:8, a double-minded man is "unstable in all his ways" (ESV).

WOUNDS, LIES, VOWS, AND STRONGHOLDS

In trying to understand the relationship between pockets of pain and the beliefs that keep us from the peace of God, I teach a model I call WLVS.[4] It looks like the word WOLVES without the vowels. I also think of it as WLVS: The Demonic Radio Network—Broadcasting All Deception, All the Time.

WLVS stands for wounds, lies, vows, and strongholds. The model works like this. When my heart gets wounded (and it happens to all of us), it creates a pocket of pain. My wounded heart will find it easier to believe the devil's lies than God's truth. So the devil is able to plant his lies in the wounded parts of my heart. These lies create a wedge between me and God. I no longer trust God in this area of pain. Instead, I vow to take control of my life. A vow is an "I will" statement about how I am going to keep myself from further pain. I say things like:

- "I will never let anyone tell me what to do."
- "I will never trust a woman again."
- "I will never put myself in a position of weakness."
- "I will prove that I am worth something."

These wounds, lies, and vows result in strongholds. A stronghold is an area of my life in which I am enslaved to something. The breakthrough I need will always involve tearing down strongholds.

Early in my ministry, a young lady came to see me because she was depressed. After a few sessions, I sensed there was something deeper going on that I had not uncovered. She agreed to go with me to see someone with more experience. The man we went to see understood the need to get to root issues and not just deal with surface problems.

Instead of dealing with her depression directly, he went searching for a root issue that was driving her depression.

As the two of them talked, she confessed to a sin she had kept secret for several years. He walked her through a prayer to receive God's forgiveness for what she had done and a prayer to forgive herself. Working together, they evicted any demons that had taken advantage not only of the sin involved, but the lies she had come to believe that were driving her depression.

That night, I watched someone transform right in front of my eyes. On the drive back, she was so happy she sang praise songs to God with joy on her face.

DECEPTION

One of the reasons deception is so hard to recognize is that it is often more about hiding elements of the truth than making up something that is totally untrue. In this sense, deception is like a magic trick or an illusion. When the magician has his assistant step into a box and two seconds later she disappears, it looks like magic. We have been deceived by the facts we know. We saw her get into the box. We saw him open the box. We saw that the box was empty. All of these things are true. When we add them up, we arrive at the conclusion that he magically made her disappear. It is not until other facts are revealed that we see what really happened.

In the same way, many of us struggle with feelings of worthlessness but do not see the deception. We are blind to it, because our thoughts include experiences that are true. It may be true that we have disappointed people. It may be true that others have told us we are worthless. We may have done things of which we are ashamed. But there are other facts that paint a different picture. The devil's job is to blind us to the facts that might get us to embrace the truth that God loves us and delights in us.

In my own journey, I have often struggled with the feeling that I am a disappointment. Many people know what it is like to feel like a fraud. We are afraid people think we are better than we are because we know how much we still struggle and how many gaps we are still trying to fill. When I was trying to decide whether or not to start a ministry called Deeper Walk, I remember telling God, "I feel like I am going to disappoint people. I know I still have a long way to go to have the kind of intimacy with You and trust that I want to have. I don't feel worthy to run an organization called Deeper Walk because it sounds like I've arrived and have everything figured out." At that point, I had a clear, distinct thought that I took as the Holy Spirit, *I'm not asking you to be perfect. I am asking you to go on a journey and invite others to join you. Can you do that?* I said yes, and God has used this mininstry to help a lot of people.

The devil has not stopped attacking my thought life. I still have holes to fill and battles to fight, but it helps to understand how deception works. Just because I can make a case for why God or others might be disappointed in me, doesn't mean that is the way God sees things.

BOLD LIES

Not all deception is about hiding important truth. Sometimes lies are bold. A counselor once invited me to sit in on a session because her client had some warfare issues going on. It didn't take long to see that she wasn't kidding. A young man dressed in black entered the room. He mocked Jesus as a weakling and boasted that the demons within him were far more powerful than the God I served. This was a bold lie. The demons were saying they were stronger than Jesus and had no fear of Him.

I asked if he would be okay with inviting Jesus to do battle with the demons inside of him. If he was right, Jesus should be no threat. He enthusiastically agreed to the contest and invited Jesus to do battle. It took about one second. With a startled look he said, "Well, that was fast. I guess Jesus isn't such a wimp."

Situations like these have taught me that Satan often lies boldly. He told this man that demons were stronger than Jesus. That is a bold lie. He told him that he was a demon, and he was starting to believe it. But it was another bold lie.

When it comes to bold lies, we have to identify them, and replace them with truth. It is also a good idea to command the spirits telling those lies to leave in the name of Jesus.

UNLEASHING THE TRANSFORMATIVE POWER OF TRUTH

Our beliefs have amazing power. One need look no further than the phenomenon of placebos. It is remarkable how often a placebo has the same impact as an actual medication. In multiple studies, 54 percent of patients reported the same level of improvement when given a placebo as when given aspirin. Perhaps even more amazing is that multiple studies showed 56 percent of patients reporting the same level of improvement when given a placebo and morphine.[5] The point here is not that placebos are just as good as medicine. The point is that there is an amazing connection between what we believe and how we feel—physically as well as emotionally.

As we have seen, false beliefs create emotional bondage. The flip side of this is that truth sets us free and transforms:

Romans 12:2—Be transformed by the renewing of your minds.
John 8:32—The truth will set you free.
John 17:17—Sanctify them by your truth.
Philippians 4:8—Whatever is good . . . think on these things.

Many of the strategies listed in this book deal with false beliefs at some level. Dealing with demons is often about renouncing the lies they tell us, and tearing down the deceptive strongholds they build. Listening to the Spirit is intended to guide us into truth as well as a deeper attachment to God. The point of this chapter has been to make it clear how powerful beliefs can be and why it is so important to take our thoughts captive and make them obedient to God.

Before we go to the next chapter, in which we explore an engine even more powerful than beliefs, let me leave you with one tool I have found helpful in dealing with false beliefs. It is a simple T-bar chart combined with listening prayer.

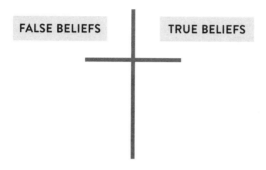

Under "false beliefs," ask God to bring to your mind one lie the enemy is trying to get you to believe and write it down. Then under "true beliefs" ask God what the truth is that needs to replace the lie. It is okay to just do one belief at a time. As you do this regularly, God will begin to expose the pattern of lies that the enemy routinely tells you, and you will begin to build a "tower of truth" to replace the stronghold of enemy lies.

I have used this tool or something like it hundreds of times. One couple who was in pain over the direction their son was going in life used this process effectively. They asked God, "In words or pictures, how does the enemy want us to picture our son?" They both got clear answers about what a horrible person he had become. As they thought about the images and words that came to mind, they felt disgust for their son.

Then they asked, "In words or pictures, God, how do You want us to see our son?" Immediately, there were tears as they both saw a precious treasure worth fighting for. They then renounced the false beliefs and commanded the spirits behind those beliefs to leave, and thanked God for showing them the truth. The false beliefs about their son had all the earmarks of the devil's work and those false beliefs needed to be exposed. Knowing the truth set them free to pursue a more life-giving path of interacting with their child.

CHAPTER 8

INCREASE YOUR JOY BONDS

YEARS AGO, there was a classic experiment called Rat Park.[1] In this experiment, the researchers got several rats addicted to drugs. An addicted rat could make his way through a maze and find a dispenser with a morphine solution in it. That didn't really surprise anyone. The big surprise came when they took an addicted rat and put him in an environment filled with other rats and filled with the sorts of things rats like. The same kind of feeder with the same morphine solution was available in this "rat paradise," but the addicted rats routinely chose relational connection with the other rats rather than the drug.

The meaning of an experiment like this can be oversimplified, but one of the lessons clearly illustrated by the Rat Park experiment is that our craving for attachment goes deeper even than a craving for morphine. As researchers have learned, deep attachments are a crucial element in overcoming substance abuse.

Amy Hamilton Glaser is a friend who has spent many years working with addicted people. Some years ago, she routinely led groups through a session on the idea that addictions are attachments to non-relational experiences and that part of the solution is to fill our lives with enough actual relational joy that we reduce our cravings. She told me that after one session she overheard a conversation in which one man said to another, "I don't understand how this works," and his friend explained it this way:

> It's like Miss Amy said—we've got our brains bonded to drugs instead of people, and we need to bond again with people. Me? I love fishing, so I started taking my kids fishing almost every day. After a few months, I couldn't wait to see my kids every day after work, and I realized I hadn't thought about the drugs in a while.

He then asked his friend if there was a hobby he enjoyed doing and someone he enjoyed doing it with. The man thought for a minute and said, "I like to golf with my friend." He encouraged the man to give that a try and see if a few months of connecting with people didn't increase his joy and diminish his cravings.

That was a pretty good summary of what she had taught. Joy forms strong attachments, and strong attachments create a powerful identity that transforms the way we live.

ATTACHMENT

The Bible doesn't use the word *attachment*, but it uses words and metaphors about adhering, glueing, and bonding to describe relational connection. One of my favorite images is that of being grafted into the vine. An example of how the Bible emphasizes attachment without using the word can be seen in the problem of idolatry. One of the greatest sins a person could commit under the Law was idolatry.

I grew up in Indiana in the 1960s and 70s and had never seen open idol worship, so it was hard for me to wrap my head around why God was so focused on idolatry and why it seemed to be the worst sin Israel could commit. Most sermons I heard talked about idolatry as loving money, but that was about as far as it went.

Today, I realize there are at least three core problems with idolatry:

1. **Idolatry replaces God with another savior.** When we think of money as an idol, it is because we trust money to save us from our problems more than we trust God. In the same way, a person can be an idol if we put them in God's place. One young man, for example, was in love with his "dream girl." He worshiped her as the embodiment of everything he wanted in a woman. Even after marrying someone else, he often found himself fantasizing about her. It was not until he dealt with the problem as idolatry that he found freedom. He renounced making an idol of her, broke any unhealthy connections that had formed, commanded spirits related to the idolatry to leave, and asked God for a new picture of how He wanted him to see her. With that the idolatry was broken.

2. **Idolatry can involve us in the occult.** Behind idols are actual demonic spirits. When we engage in idolatry, we summon these spirits. When we participate in the rituals of idolatry, we enter agreements with demons and give them permission to a place in our life. Such idolatry needs to be broken. Idols must be destroyed, participation renounced, and spirits told to leave. One of the reasons deliverance was a common part of discipleship in the early church was that most of the converts in the Gentile world were coming to Christ from idol worship.

3. **Idolatry is a direct attack on our attachment to God.** If I have a divided heart, it means part of my heart is bonded to God and part of my heart is bonded to the world and to the demonic spirits that rule the world. Solomon had a divided heart, because part of his heart was bonded to God and part of his heart was bonded to his pagan wives and their gods. We read in 1 Kings 11:4, "As Solomon grew old, his wives turned his heart after other gods,

and his heart was not fully devoted to the Lord his God, as the heart of David his father had been."

One could make the case that the Bible's focus on the heart is a way of making attachment the core issue in life. It is at the heart level that attachments are formed. It is the heart that loves God and bonds to Him (Deut. 6:5; 11:13). Consider what Moses says about false prophets in Deuteronomy 13. One might expect that God allows false prophets to test our orthodoxy and see if we will hold on to the truth, but according to Moses, they are sent to test something deeper than orthodoxy. They are sent to test our hearts. "The Lord your God is testing you to find out *whether you love him with all your heart and with all your soul*" (Deut. 13:3, emphasis added). The point here is that false prophecy is an attachment test. Are we bonded to God with all our hearts or do we have a divided heart? A divided heart can be led astray more easily because our bond with God is weaker.

The hallmark of a false prophet was that he led people away from their attachment to God. We can recognize the false prophets in our world today because they lead us away from a pure love of God and lead us into the worship of other beings and into love of the world. From this perspective, a verse like Proverbs 4:23, which warns us to guard our hearts above all things, may be talking less about the beliefs we let into our minds, and more about the attachments we allow our hearts to form.

No doubt a whole book could be written just about the theology of attachment in the Bible.

BONDING AND THE BRAIN

Bonding is foundational to brain function. The deepest part of our brain is devoted to attachment, and the primary function of the right hemisphere of the brain is also attachment. The right side of our brain is basically a bonding engine. One has to believe God did this on purpose. It is a clue to what He values and considers most important.

Not only is bonding the deepest part of brain function, it is more powerful than beliefs when it comes to how we live. Peer pressure is a powerful force. Aligning ourselves with the group in order to belong often overwhelms what we believe to be true. Like sheep, we follow the crowd no matter where it is going.

According to Dr. Emily Falk at the University of Pennsylvania, "People care about what others think across all different age groups— and that influences how much they value different ideas and behaviors."[2] In his book *Living Above the Level of Mediocrity*, Chuck Swindoll tells the story of a psychologist who conducted an experiment in which ten students at a time were brought into a room for a test. Each group of ten was instructed to point to the longest line on three separate charts. However, nine of the ten students had been instructed to vote for the second longest line each time. Only one person in each group was not in on the test. The point of the test was to see if peer pressure would cause people to vote for something that was obviously false. In 75 percent of the cases—from small children to high school students—people voted with the group even when they knew they were wrong.[3] Stories like this help us understand the bonds often play an even greater role than beliefs in driving the way we live.

In our book *Rare Leadership*, Jim Wilder and I describe the attachment engine in the brain as the joy elevator.[4] I introduced this term earlier in the book, but now I want to take a closer look at how it works.

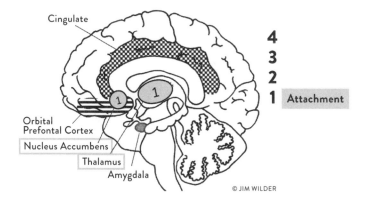

1. Attachment

In the diagram above, you should see the terms nucleus *accumbens* and *thalamus*. These two parts of the brain are the key players in the attachment center or first floor of the joy elevator. The nucleus accumbens is the source of our deep cravings, and what it craves most are joy-filled relationships. Just as the rats in Rat Park craved attachment with their family and friends over morphine, so our core cravings are relational. We love to be attached to people who are happy to be with us. However, when this part of our brains cannot attach to someone who is safe and happy to be with us, it will form attachments to non-relational substitutes. This is how addictions form. We bond to non-relational substitutes instead of bonding in joy to God or people.

The attachment light. The "first floor" of the brain functions like a light bulb. It comes on when we feel like bonding with someone who is happy to see us. We see this when babies search diligently for the eyes of someone who is happy to see them. Once they make the connection, they light up with joy and often giggle and coo with delight. The attachment center at the base of the brain is what drives that desire to bond. It makes the light come on.

When our natural desire to attach is ignored or is greeted with anger or disgust, it creates problems. Fear begins to mold the way our attachment light operates instead of joy. The result is that we will learn to bond to others in fear and it will be hard to form bonds that are anchored in joy. I will have more to say about fear bonds at the end of the chapter.

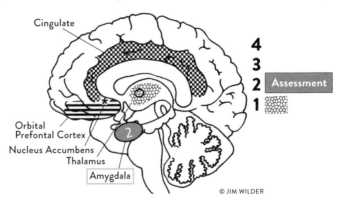

2. Assessment

The second floor of the joy elevator is where our attachments are assessed. When the attachment light on the first floor lights up because something is personal to me, it is then scanned by the amygdala (see the previous diagram) to see if the situation is good, bad, or scary.

As mentioned in an earlier chapter, the amygdala is often referred to as the source of our "fight or flight" response. While this is true, there is more going on. According to Dr. Wilder, the amygdala is only capable of three assessments: (1) This is good, (2) This is bad, or (3) This is scary.[5] When the amygdala reacts to something as scary, it triggers the high-energy reactions of fight (anger) or flight (fear). However, when it assesses something as bad, it triggers the opposite reaction. It produces the low-energy emotions of shame, sadness, despair, or disgust.

The Big Six Negative Emotions

© JIM WILDER

As I wrote earlier in this book, our emotional capacity is directly related to our brain's ability to handle the signals sent out by the amygdala. The amygdala may send a strong fear signal to the body that pushes us beyond our window of tolerance. When this happens, we lose the ability to act like ourselves and our non-relational brain takes over. However, if we have developed enough capacity, the amygdala can send the same signal to the body without overwhelming us. We may feel a spike in our emotions, but not enough to cause a brain cramp that knocks our relational circuits offline. We are able to regulate our emotions, which allows us to act like ourselves despite how we feel.

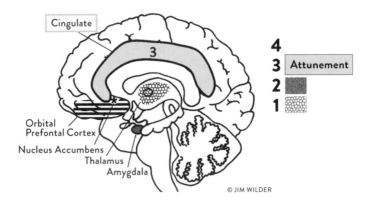

© JIM WILDER

3. Attunement

The third floor of the joy elevator is attunement. When I talk about our higher-level brain functions, I am referring to the third and fourth floors of the joy elevator. The third floor allows me to read my environment and recognize what needs my attention. The fourth floor allows my true, relational self to stay in charge even when bad or scary things happen.

The attunement center is a description of the cingulate cortex. This part of the brain functions like radar that is always operating in the background. It "reads" my environment and people to help me know when I am safe or in danger, and to recognize the subtle clues that inform my view of reality.

When my attunement center is functioning well, I read people clearly. This helps me synchronize with their emotions and connect with them. If two of us "read" each other's body language correctly, we can share a lot of nonverbal information with each other. We can send and receive signals that let us know we like each other, or we are attracted to each other, or we are disgusted by the situation we are in, or that one of us is afraid but the other is at peace. There are almost no end of options here. To the extent that we can tune in and read each other well, we can share what is called a *mutual mind state*.

A mutual mind state is one in which we carry on a nonverbal conversation. For example, if my wife and I are talking and one of our kids walks in the room, just a glance from one of us can communicate a lot. It can communicate, "I'm happy to see you, but now is not a good time for you to be here." Or it can communicate a dozen other reactions. Such nonverbal communication lies at the heart of most of our relationships.

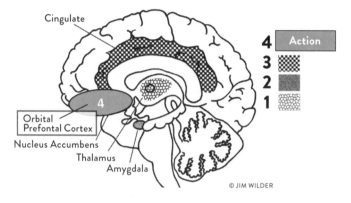

© JIM WILDER

4. Action

In *Rare Leadership in the Workplace*, Dr. Jim Wilder and I refer to the fourth (top) floor of the joy elevator as the *action center*.[6] In this book, I have been calling it either the *identity center* or the *joy center*. It is the joy center because it is the part of the brain that grows with the experience of joy, and it is the identity center because it is the part of the brain that remembers who we are and how it is like us to act. It is the action center because it is the part of the brain we want in command and controlling how we act. The technical term for this part of the brain in the diagram above is the orbital prefrontal cortex.

This is the part of our brain we want in charge when problems arise. It controls functions related to the following activities:

- Identity—It allows us to remember who we are and how it is like us to act.

- Motivation—It remembers the values that drive the way we live.
- Emotional control—It helps us regulate our emotions so they don't overwhelm us.
- Ability to focus—It helps us solve problems by making sure our best self is on the job.
- Relational skills—This is not the ability to be charming. This is the ability to remain relational and act like yourself no matter the situation.
- Care for others—This activity grows directly out of seeing others as "my people" or at least seeing them in a category of protection (as opposed to "enemy").
- Conscience—We can only live without a conscience when we leave the action center and start operating in enemy mode from a different part of our brain. The good news is that when we operate out of the relational part of our brain, our conscience shows up automatically.[7]

We can tell when the relational part of our brain is in control because we remain curious, keep relationships bigger than problems, enjoy appreciation, and feel peace more easily. Jim Wilder writes, "The better trained and stronger our executive brain has become the more we can keep the executive functions working well during times of stress, problems, and upset."[8]

LEFT
Narrative Engine

RIGHT
Joy Elevator

5. *The Narrative Engine*

When most of us think about the brain, we think about our ability to reason and solve problems. We equate it with knowledge, intelligence, and our thought life. However, most of these activities are happening on the left side of our brain, and they only get activated after the joy elevator on the right side of the brain has processed what is happening to us faster than we have time to think about it.

When my brain is stuck at one of the four levels of the joy elevator, it is harder for my left brain to think clearly. As a result, I don't do my best thinking or problem-solving when my emotions have pushed me beyond my emotional capacity. If my joy elevator gets stuck because the bad or scary signals being sent by the amygdala cause me to lose access to the higher-level brain functions, the engine on the left side of my brain often jumps in and tries to solve the problem. That may sound like a good idea, but it is trying to solve the problem without all of the data and without access to my identity center. Thus, I will jump to a lot of wrong conclusions.

Psychiatrist Karl Lehman refers to the narrative engine on the left side of the brain as our "verbal logical explainer" or VLE.[9] The idea behind the VLE is that our left brain will put into words (verbal) the simplest logical explanation it can. However, logic does not lead to truth when it is built on wrong data. I heard this illustrated by a preacher years ago who made the following completely logical but utterly false statement:

Nothing is more important than obedience.
A donut hole is nothing.
Therefore, a donut hole is more important than obedience.

As you can see, the simplest logical explanation is not always the right one. Perhaps you see a red-bearded man walk past you on the street and feel a sudden sense of anxiety. Your narrative engine (VLE) will immediately try to interpret why you felt this emotion, but if it doesn't have all the data it needs, there is a good chance it will come up with the wrong answer.

When our brains function well, and our joy elevator is running smoothly, it is not hard to live with peace and joy. But a malfunction at any one of the five levels of brain function will impact every level above it. If the attachment light on the first floor is not behaving properly, it will skew the function of the entire elevator. If the assessment center on the second floor sends a bad or scary signal that overwhelms the system, it will make it hard to act like ourselves and think clearly. If we lose access to our ability to read people well, it will change the way we feel about people.

What the joy elevator teaches us is that God designed the brain to run on the fuel of joyful attachment. He wants us to know the peace that comes from having safe, secure attachments and the joy that helps us feel like ourselves. However, when our brain isn't operating the way God designed it, we don't form joy bonds. We form fear bonds.

JOY BONDS VERSUS FEAR BONDS

Joy bonds and fear bonds are largely about motivation. If we are motivated to spend time with someone or perform some task out of fear of what will happen if we don't, that is a fear bond. If we are motivated to spend time with someone or perform some task out of the joy that will result, that is a joy bond.

For example, you can go to your child's school play out of fear of what people will think of you if you don't. To change that fear motivation into a joyful motivation, you need to go into problem-solving mode and get a new perspective. Instead of going to your child's performance because you are afraid of your wife's reaction if you don't, because you are afraid of what others will think, or you are afraid you will somehow mess up your child's life by not being there, you need to find something about going to the school play that will bring you joy. Perhaps you can look forward to sharing your child's joy, seeing your wife's smile, or connecting with someone else who will be there. If you can't find any joy to motivate you, then you will be stuck living out of fear.

This applies to nearly everything we do. We can motivate ourselves with joy or motivate ourselves with fear. Most of us are predisposed to do one or the other based on how we were raised and how well our joy elevator is functioning. But one of the ways we can train ourselves to form joy bonds rather than fear bonds is by working on our perspective. We need to learn to catch ourselves using fear as our motivator and focus on joyful motivators instead. The more we do this, the more it becomes a habit.

As the leader of a ministry, I often catch myself saying things like, "If we don't sell more books, we won't be able to pay the staff." Or, "If we don't get more people to sign up for this event, we may have to cancel." Those are both true statements, but they are fear motivators. What I am learning to do, instead, is to replace those fear statements with joy statements. I may say something like, "If we sell more books, not only will it help pay the bills, but it will get our message to more people and that means more changed lives." I may end up taking exactly the same steps to sell more books, but doing it out of joy rather than fear changes everything about the experience.

As a husband, I can motivate myself to spend time with my wife out of fear or out of joy. I can tell myself, "She's going to be mad if I don't get home on time." But if that is my only motivation, it isn't going to do much to increase the joy in our relationship. However, if I tell myself, "I am looking forward to spending time with my wife and doing something that will make her smile," I will still try to get home on time, but now I am doing it out of joy rather than fear.

FEAR BONDS

When we don't develop safe, secure attachments as children, our brains learn to make fear our normal source of motivation. Instead of seeking joy in our relationships, we focus on damage control and pain management. The problem is that the more we motivate ourselves with fear, the more distorted our approach to life becomes and the less emotional health we experience.

According to the Life Model, there are three core types of fear bonds: dismissive, distracted, and disorganized.[10] The following descriptions rely heavily on a series of blogs on the topic written by Life Model contributor Maribeth Poole.[11]

1. Dismissive Attachment

Dismissive attachment is the result of an attachment light that has learned not to come on because it is not likely anyone will respond. This leads to developing an avoidant lifestyle. We become emotional Teflon. People just don't seem to stick.

As infants or toddlers, when we crave joyful attachment and no one responds, our brains notice and react. If I look for happy eyes and find none, if I cry out and no one responds, if I get no reaction regardless of my desperation, the attachment light in my brain will learn not to bother coming on. As my attachment light learns to light up less and less often, a dismissive attachment style begins to form. This underactive attachment light keeps us from seeking joyful attachment even when it is available.

Dismissive fear bonds are formed as a means of protection against the pain of being ignored. In order to change this pattern, we will need to intentionally "wake up" our joy light. This often means facing some of our relational fears and doing things we have always feared will cost us relational connection.

For example, I grew up in a Christian subculture that frowned on using poker cards. The cards themselves were associated with gambling, and using them was seen as worldly. Fear of rejection by the group kept me from ever using them even if I wasn't gambling. This may seem like a small thing, but many of us live our entire lives out of fear of what others will think of us and follow self-imposed rules God has not established, Facing some of these fears can help us transform a dismissive bond into a healthier joy bond.

2. Distracted Attachment

Distracted attachment is the result of an attachment light that gets stuck in the *on* position most of the time. If, as a little one, I am never sure of when someone will respond to my searching eyes or my cries for attention, my brain will learn to keep the attachment light on all the time—just in case. This overactive attachment light tends to make us clingy and needy.

People with distracted attachment tend to be anxious. They also tend to give their attention to whoever or whatever is the scariest or most urgent at any given time. In her blog "Distracted David," Maribeth Poole shares some of the following observations about distracted people:

- Unless someone is in crisis or something is urgent, a distracted person may not pay attention to that person or situation.
- Distracted people often attach to someone they see as able to meet their needs and can become paralyzed and nonfunctional when problems arise in those relationships.
- Preoccupation with the urgent matters that distract this person often causes them to be unreliable, because they tend to ignore responsibilities because of their focus on the crisis of the moment.
- Distracted people often have a secret—a guilty pleasure they hide from others. They have an addiction they hide from others and wish they could break, because they know it is not a reflection of who they really are.[12]

Distracted people are generally raised by distracted parents who are inconsistently (and unpredictably) available for our emotional needs. We often only get our parents' undivided attention when there is a crisis. As a result, a profound inner angst develops that is unsure my needs will be met, thus creating an anxious personality.

3. Disorganized Attachment

Disorganized attachment develops when my attachment light is unsure when it is safe to light up and when it is dangerous. If, as an infant or toddler, the same person who does joy workouts with me also hurts me and possibly abuses me, it creates an intolerable internal conflict. My attachment light is never sure when it is safe to come on. This overwhelming confusion makes it impossible to develop a reliable pattern of emotional regulation, and I tend to be emotionally volatile and unstable.

People with disorganized attachment can present themselves in a responsible and friendly way that leaves us with no idea of the war that is raging below the surface. But the surface calm can't last. Chaos inevitably comes to rule their relationships and their emotions.

It is important for us to develop the self-awareness to recognize the fear-bonding patterns in our lives. Recognizing our bonding style helps us recognize why we feel the way we do and can help us remember to adopt new strategies in our relationships. Our goal is to move toward a secure attachment pattern in which we develop the skills to regulate our emotions and develop our capacity to attach to God and others with a clear understanding of our value.

Can I Have More Than One Fear-Bond Pattern?

The quick answer to this question is yes. Some of us are firmly locked into one of these patterns, but all of us can adopt different fear-bonding patterns situationally.

For example, I can see elements of all three fear-bonding patterns in my life. When I get really overwhelmed, I can exhibit disorganized tendencies. I can feel chaotic and out of control inside. At other times, I can be dismissive. My joy light simply doesn't blaze very brightly even when it should. Most of the time, however, I am distracted. Whatever is most troubling gets my attention.

When I first learned about these types of fear bonds, I thought I was dismissive. I could see it as a family pattern and recognized it in myself. However, one day both my wife and my daughter read Maribeth Poole's blogs and had the same reaction. They told me, "You aren't dismissive. You are distracted." It turns out they were right. My dominant pattern was to give them focused attention when I had to help with a problem. If one of them was distressed, they got my undivided attention. Otherwise,

I was pretty dismissive. It helped my self-awareness tremendously to recognize this pattern in my behavior. It allowed me to recognize more quickly when our attachment patterns were clashing and what needed to change.

Fear Bonds and God

If fear bonds and joy bonds are about motivation, then we need to ask ourselves: *What motivates us to have a relationship with God? Are we in a relationships simply so we can avoid hell? Do we try to please God so we won't get in trouble, or is there joy to be had in any part of the relationship?* One of the reasons many of us struggle to feel close to God is that we are fear bonded to Him.

I have learned that our dominant attachment style (whether joyful, dismissive, distracted, or disorganized) will impact the way we bond to God. If forming joy bonds is easy and normal for us, it will be much more natural for us to form a joy bond with God. However, if we are dismissive with people, we will tend to be dismissive with God. He just never feels close, and we rarely expect Him to be available to us. If we are distracted, we will ignore God for long stretches of time until we have a crisis, then He will suddenly become the most important person in our life. If we are disorganized, we may want a close connection with God, but will instinctively distrust Him and fear even trying to get close.

In her book *Taking Every Thought Captive*, Dr. Alaine Pakkala introduces many of her chapters with sample prayers of how people with disorganized attachment tend to view God.[13] One prayer might begin, "God, I think you are cruel and couldn't care less about me." Another prayer might start, "God, it feels like you are a million miles away." She also points out that many people with significant father wounds find it nearly impossible to pray to God as "Father." So, she often suggests that highly traumatized people pray to "the Good Shepherd" instead. As she often points out, very few people she knows were abused by shepherds, so it is usually a less triggering image.

The point here is that if we have developed a dismissive, distracted, or disorganized approach to bonding with humans, we will bring that same attachment problem to our walk with God. I have seen this in my own life. Sometimes my attachment light just doesn't come on, and I don't really feel like spending time with God. Sometimes, I am overwhelmed by need and feel a desperation to connect. At other times, I start to bond to God but get distracted by shiny objects in my environment. For other people, God feels dangerous. If they went through the kind of abuse that creates disorganized attachment, God will feel very scary—even cruel. Trusting Him is not simply a choice they are able to make until a lot of work gets done. In each case, transforming our attachment patterns with people will help us transform our attachment pattern with God.

HOW DO WE CHANGE FEAR BONDS TO JOY BONDS?

There are three keys to changing fear bonds into joy bonds. All of them have been introduced in this book already.

1. **We need to change our self-talk.** We need to recognize when we are motivating ourselves with fear, and replace fearful motivations with joyful ones. To do this, we need to monitor our self-talk and intentionally find reasons to do what we do that produce joy.

2. **We need to develop our brain's capacity for joy by doing joy workouts.** Joy workouts are about sharing joy and experiencing rest with someone else. The more often we experience joy and rest with another person or a group of people, the faster we can grow the infrastructure in our brain related to joy.

3. **We need to increase our ability to return to joy from upset emotions with bounce workouts.** You may recall that bounce workouts have to do with developing our ability to recover from upsetting emotions. A key tool in this process is learning to tell stories about times you felt a negative emotion but recovered or acted like yourself. Like joy workouts, bounce workouts need to be done with other people.

If you want these steps as an acrostic, you can use JOBS—Joy Workouts, Observing Fear Motivators, Bounce Workouts, Self-Talk Corrections.

I hope this chapter has helped you better understand the role of bonds in driving our emotions. Belonging, peer pressure, joy bonds, and fear bonds are all powerful forces in shaping how we feel and how we live.

In the next two chapters, we will transition from the physical engines (body, beliefs, bonds) to the spiritual engines (Spirit and wicked spirits). The next strategy we will explore is listening to the Spirit. For some of you this is common habit, for others it may be a new idea. Either way, I hope you will find the explanations and guidance helpful.

CHAPTER 9

LISTEN TO THE SPIRIT

TRICIA HAD A SECRET.[1] She hadn't told anyone what had happened at the church picnic when she was a little girl. After attending a seminar based on my book *Understanding the Wounded Heart*, Tricia made an appointment to see me. She wasn't there to talk about her secret. She was there because she lived with a lot of fear, shame, and despair and was hoping for a breakthrough.

She told me her story, and there were all sorts of relevant issues that might have explained her feelings, but she did not tell me the secret. When she got to the end of her story, I asked her to go through a simple exercise in listening prayer. She asked, "Father, if there is a root memory fueling my current problems, would You bring it to my mind right now?" That is when the Holy Spirit showed up. It was subtle. She didn't have a dramatic encounter or a supernatural manifestation. He simply reminded her of that day at the picnic and brought that root memory into focus. With her eyes still closed in prayer, she said, "I've never told anyone this before." I knew at that moment something special was about to happen. If someone trusts you enough to tell you something they have never told anyone before, something important is happening.

She went on to tell me about an older boy and some unwanted touching. She remembered being a little afraid but also curious and excited. But the longer it went on, the more she wanted it to stop, and he wouldn't stop. She began to feel very afraid and, afterward, very dirty. She looked up at me with tears in her eyes. She looked very young.

I led her to ask the Spirit to bring to her mind any lies from the enemy that started to feel true because of that event. She closed her eyes again and repeated the prayer. Then she said:

- I believed I was dirty and could never be clean again.
- I believed the only thing anyone liked about me was my body.
- I believed if anyone found out I would be rejected forever.
- I believed God hated me.
- I believed God let me down.
- I believed my life was over.

These thoughts weren't running through her head on the day her trauma happened. But they were all thoughts that began to feel true after that day. As you look at the list, you can see how much weight she was carrying and why she struggled with fear, shame, and despair. There was also some anger there too, and the roots of a hidden rift with God. Like most people with pain in their past, the wound had given the devil an opportunity to plant lies that made it hard to believe God really loved her.

Tricia wanted to be a good Christian, but she struggled to feel close to God. She never felt like she measured up, and no matter how hard she tried, she never felt God was really happy with her or even happy to see her.

Once we had written out a clear list of beliefs that were anchored in this memory, I asked her to rate how true they felt on a scale of one to ten. They all felt like at least a ten to her. Tricia then prayed a simple prayer, "Jesus, I invite You to do whatever You need to do to heal this memory." I told her to revisit her memory in her mind and tell me if anything changed. Did she feel different? Did she see anything different? Did something feel true that didn't feel true before?

With a bit of surprise in her voice, Tricia said, "I'm not sure what to think about this. I see Jesus standing next to me, and He is angry. He's not angry at me. He is angry with that boy." Suddenly, she covered her mouth with her hand and said, "Oh my, Jesus just shoved him into the creek."[2] Then she laughed. The boy who had been so scary just a moment before looked a bit ridiculous, and she felt no more fear when she thought about him. She then let me know that Jesus looked her in the eyes and said, "No one has the right to do that to you. You are precious. You are My princess." With a smile on her face, she let me know that Jesus had started to dance with her the way a proud father would dance with his little girl.

God used a simple listening prayer exercise to completely heal Tricia's memory and set her free from multiple controlling beliefs and emotions. The Holy Spirit stripped this memory of its power and gave it new meaning. When Tricia and I walked back through the list of lies that felt like "tens" just a few minutes before, they all felt like "zeroes." The truth had set her free. The Spirit also used the opportunity to help this young woman form a joy bond with Jesus for the first time in her life.

This story is a compilation of multiple experiences I have witnessed and represents the kind of miraculous healing that only the Holy Spirit can do. In most situations like this, controlling beliefs that felt completely true before the Holy Spirit did His work felt completely untrue in a matter of minutes.

Someone may ask, "How do you know this was God and not just the girl's imagination?" Good question. The simple answer is that I don't know. What I do know is that when biblical truth became more real to people like Tricia, their level of peace grew and the fruit of the Spirit increased. So, whether it was literally God or simply Spirit-led imagination, it produced good fruit.

HEARING GOD'S VOICE

Most of us are attracted to stories like these for obvious reasons. Who wouldn't want to experience a breakthrough of this magnitude in one prayer session? So, let me temper this just a bit. For some people who have a lot of emotional capacity and a good support system in place, an event like this can be the breakthrough that changes everything for many years to come. But a person with layers and layers of issues and a lot of A trauma may require dozens more sessions like this one and help related to all five of the emotional engines described in this book if they are to reach a new level of wholeness.

In a previous chapter, I talked about the dangers of the New Age movement, and listening prayer is another area where that danger exists. Some people who have tried to hear from God have been deceived and led into counterfeit experiences. Because of this, it is easy for some to dismiss the practice altogether. However, it is hard to deny that the Bible frequently refers to God appearing to people and speaking to people. It is also true that many heroes of the faith extolled the merits of learning to hear God's voice:

- A. W. Tozer, in his classic book *The Pursuit of God*, writes, "Lord, teach me to listen. The times are noisy and my ears are weary with the thousand raucous sounds which continuously assault them. Give me the spirit of the boy Samuel when he said to Thee, 'Speak, for thy servant heareth.' Let me hear Thee speaking in my heart. Let me get used to the sound of Thy Voice, that its tones may be familiar when the sounds of earth die away and the only sound will be the music of Thy speaking Voice. Amen."[3]

- Henry Blackaby, in *Experiencing God*—his bestselling book with Claude King—writes, "The testimony of the Bible from Genesis to Revelation is that God speaks to His people. In our day, God communicates with us through the Holy Spirit."[4]

- Charles Spurgeon gave a sermon in 1875 titled "How to Converse with God,"[5] in which he tells of a variety of ways God uses Scripture to awaken something in us that we recognize as God's voice. Spurgeon here limits hearing from God to sensing His guidance through Scripture, but Scripture itself does not limit hearing God's voice to something that only happens by reading Scripture.

The use of listening prayer is a common practice for many evangelical counselors[6] and has been taught by groups like the Navigators (see Rusty Rustenbach's book, *A Guide for Listening and Inner Healing Prayer: Inviting God into the Broken Places*) and was a main point of ministry at the 2022 Urbana Conference.[7]

A THEOLOGY OF THE SPIRIT

The Holy Spirit is mentioned in the opening verses of Scripture. He is associated with life, power, and wisdom.

Life

The Hebrew word for *Spirit* is the same word that means *breath*. You can see a strong connection between breath and life. We wait for a baby to take their first breath of air as a sign that they have successfully made the transition from the unseen world of the womb into the visible world of living, breathing humanity. Our lifespans are often looked at from first breath to last breath. Adam was just a lump of clay until God's breath entered him and he came to life (Gen. 2:7). In Ezekiel 37, a dead army is brought back to life in three stages: first their bones are reassembled, then their bones are covered with flesh, and finally, God's breath enters them and they come to life. In a similar way, in the New Testament, we are all dead in our sins until God's Spirit enters us. It is the breath of God that causes us to be "born again" (John 3:7) and without the Spirit we are spiritually dead (Rom. 8:9).

All of this points to the idea that life in the Spirit is crucial to Christianity. If the Spirit is our life, then we experience that life most fully when we are walking in the Spirit. We experience only a dim reflection of that life when we are walking according to the flesh.

Power

The church was born in an outpouring of Holy Spirit power, and demonstrations of the Spirit's power routinely accompanied the introduction of the gospel to new communities. Thus, Paul reminded the Corinthians that his preaching was not with wise and persuasive words of human wisdom but with a demonstration of the Spirit's power (1 Cor. 2:4). Paul also appealed to the memory of the Spirit's power when writing to the Galatians (Gal. 3:5) and Thessalonians (1 Thess. 1:4–5).

Thousands of people around the world have left false religions and started to follow Jesus because the Holy Spirit healed someone they knew or they received a dream in which Jesus was revealed to them or some other supernatural manifestation of the Spirit's power led to their conversion. I have talked to some of these people directly. In many cultures, power speaks louder than truth. People know the devil has power. They know the witchdoctors have power. It is not until they see the power of God that they are willing to embrace Christ.[8]

I met a man whose wife (prior to their marriage) had served as something like an undercover police officer whose job was enforcing the rules of the national religion.[9] However, her mother was terminally ill and she herself was becoming overwhelmed with depression. The mother did the unthinkable and called a Christian TV show. A miracle happened and the mother was completely healed of her disease. When she went to the doctor to confirm her healing, the doctor asked which spiritual leader had performed the healing. The young woman whose mother had been healed said, "Jesus." As soon as she confessed the name of Jesus publically, she felt something change inwardly. That was the beginning of her journey and she continues to serve Christ to this day.[10]

There are two common actions attributed to the Spirit in

Scripture—anointing and filling. To *anoint* is to be poured out and cover someone. This image of anointing is routinely associated with an experience of the Spirit's power. For example, when the Spirit came upon Samson, he was given super-strength (Judg. 14:6, 19; 15:14). It leads us to imagine a person who wasn't naturally overpowering (the way he is usually portrayed), but someone who—under the control of the Spirit—was unbeatable.

In Northern Europe, there were people called *berserkers* who had a counterfeit form of this. They would be possessed by a spirit and become virtually unstoppable.[11] There is a similar counterpart to this in Asia. I talked to a man who watched a person literally grow muscle mass in front of his eyes and perform superhuman acts of strength because of the spirit that took control of him. Later, he led this man through deliverance and evicted the spirit that did this to him. This modern-day berserker lost his power, but regained his mental and emotional stability and was able to form a deep connection to Jesus.

Wisdom

Whereas the anointing of the Spirit tends to refer to an outpouring of the Spirit's power, to be filled with the Spirit is routinely associated with wisdom. For example, the lead craftsman of the tabernacle was said to have wisdom because the Spirit of God was in him (Ex. 31:2–5; 35:31). Both Joseph and Daniel had the wisdom to interpret dreams because they were filled with the Spirit of God (Gen. 41:38; Dan. 5:11, 14). When Peter stood on trial before the Sanhedrin, he knew what to say because he was filled with the Spirit who gave him the wisdom he needed (Acts 4:8). Stephen was full of wisdom because he was filled with the Spirit (Acts 6:3). Thus, the Sanhedrin could not stand against his Spirit-led wisdom when he defended himself at his trial (Acts 6:10).

The Holy Spirit is called the Spirit of wisdom (Deut. 34:9; Isa. 11:2). In Ephesians 1:17, Paul prayed that his readers would be given the Spirit of wisdom and revelation. It seems in context that he was not praying for them to receive the Spirit for the first time, but that through their growing intimacy with God, the eyes of their hearts would be opened, and the Spirit's wisdom would be revealed to them more clearly.

WALKING IN THE SPIRIT—A LIFESTYLE

The Christian life can be summed up as walking in the Spirit. In other words, the life God wants for us has, at its core, an intimate relationship with Him in which we experience access to His wisdom and His power through the Holy Spirit. Now, that sounds almost too good to be true—especially if we imagine that it is a recipe for being happy all the time and getting all of our prayers answered quickly with a yes. But we need look no further than "the hall of faith" in Hebrews 11 or the life of Christ or the life of Paul to see that a life of intimacy with God and access to His wisdom and power is not a recipe for an easy life free from suffering or emotional distress. It is, however, essential to our maturity development as Christians.

If relational joy is at the heart of emotional capacity and, thus, maturity development, it makes sense that growing our capacity for relational joy with God is going to be a crucial element of an emotional healing journey. However, this is going to look different at every stage of maturity development.

Spiritual NICU Babies

Some people start their Christian journey with a burst of joy they think will never fade. Others have a much more modest entry into the faith. No matter where you start, developing a walk of faith is about learning to trust God and to remain relational with Him no matter how hard things get.

There is a common misconception that God doesn't want to see us until we get our act together. I have met with several people who were told by leaders in their churches that they needed to clean themselves up before they could come back to church or that they needed to approach God in just the right attitude of awe and respect in order for their prayers to be heard. But this has not been my experience. God would much rather we be honest with Him about our emotions—even if we are angry with Him—than to avoid Him until we could pray with the right attitude. God wants honesty not performance.

This is especially true of deeply wounded people who don't trust God at all because of the abuse they have experienced. They are not just infants in the faith, some are like Neonatal ICU (NICU) babies. Telling them to trust God and draw close to Him is no more possible than telling a baby in NICU to walk. The capacity has not yet been built for that to be an option. Sometimes people have to start with the understanding that God would rather have the relationship than the performance. He knows we are not going to grow without Him, so it would be absurd to tell someone like this they need to get their act together before a relationship with God is possible.

For example, I have met with several people who were abused in church or by religious leaders. It would be unfair to expect someone with this type of background to respond to typical advice on how to develop their walk with God. Many of them will never set foot in church again—at least not until a tremendous amount of healing takes place.

Where do you start in helping someone like this learn to walk in the Spirit? You can't just tell them to practice spiritual disciplines. At some level, you are dealing with someone who needs a new family with a spiritual mom and dad, several mentors, friends who can handle his or her extreme mood swings, a Bible teacher with a lot of patience, and people who are skilled in prayer ministry. A single counselor meeting once a week can only do so much, and many churches are happy to let someone else deal with chaos. People with this level of abuse are not just infants spiritually. They are more like preemies and need a lot of extra care.

MATURITY AND SPIRITUAL DISCIPLINE

Too many of our solutions are designed for adults and do not take into consideration the actual maturity level of the people being discipled.

This is routinely true when it comes to spiritual disciplines and traditional discipleship methods. Here are some examples of how maturity levels affect the way we teach people how to walk in the Spirit.

1. Infants Cannot Do Things for Themselves

Infants need someone else to notice what they need and do things for them. Thus, spiritual infants need to be around people and watch how they handle life, including how they pray. I was invited to be a guest speaker at a recovery ministry gathering attended by hundreds of people. At the end, there was a call to receive Christ. I was able to pray with a young lady. In the process, I did not simply have her pray the sinner's prayer, but I immediately led her to ask Jesus what He wanted her to know about the trauma that had brought her to this point. She practiced some listening prayer (not knowing that's what it was called). What she heard was spot-on and gave her a feeling of hope and peace. She felt like Jesus saw her and loved her. Since she was starting a new relationship with Jesus, I wanted her to experience that relationship and know that Jesus was there for her all the time.

I mention this story because it is easy to think that something like listening prayer is for those who are advanced in their faith. But the reality is that even non-Christians often hear from Jesus. There are many stories of people who heard Jesus speak to them before they ever crossed the line of faith. Some were even atheists, occultists, or following other religions.

Margaret Webb gave her life to Christ when she was young, but walked away from the faith later in life. She told God she wanted to know the truth . . . as long as it wasn't evangelical Christianity. Eventually she became deeply involved in the New Age movement. Then one day, God spoke to her when she least expected it and told her Jesus really was the Son of God. Even though she didn't want to hear that, it started her journey back to Jesus.

When I met Margaret, she had founded a ministry called Alive and Well that helped people encounter the Jesus of Scripture in deep and life transforming ways.

Many others have testified to seeking the god of another religion only to encounter Jesus and begin following Him.

2. Children Need Guidance on How to Pray

At the child-level of maturity development, we are learning to do things for ourselves with the goal of being able to take care of ourselves and not stay stuck in infant-level maturity so that someone else has to recognize what we need and deal with it for us. Thus, in spiritual formation, people at child-level maturity benefit greatly from having doctrinal prayers that serve as models for them.[12] It can help to have a prayer process to follow. I was raised on the ACTS prayer process—Adoration, Confession, Thanksgiving, Supplication. This is what I mean by a prayer process. It is a model that gives people tracks on which to run as they are learning to pray. Such step-by-step prayer processes are usually developed to target people who are learning how to practice spiritual disciplines for themselves.

3. Adults Need a Community to Help Their Prayer Life Thrive

To be an adult is not to be self-sufficient in the sense that we don't need anyone else. Being an adult does not mean, "God and me against the world." To be an adult means that we have developed the relational skills to bond with joy to a group. While there are seasons of isolation in most of our lives and there are very personal and individual times of prayer as adults, the issue here is that we need to be in a group that collectively makes prayer and spiritual formation a priority. When we are in a group of people who enjoy spending time together and who are all committed to growing, it is easy to thrive.

Community is like the soil in which we grow.[13] If the soil is nutrient dense—if our community is full of joy and handles conflict well—growth can happen almost automatically. However, if our community is not focused on growth, if it is not joyful, and if, in a sense, it is nutrient-light, it can be a real struggle to grow. Most of the young people I know who want a deeper walk with God struggle because they feel all alone on their journey. They don't have people who are on the path with them. As a result, they grow in spurts but suffer long periods of feeling stuck, stalled, and dissatisfied.

Some of us are stuck in communities that have an appearance of being focused on growth but in reality are toxic. They are built on fear not joy. They demand conformity to a leader who is not to be questioned. In the end, they can suck the life out of our desire to even be a Christian. There are whole movements devoted to supporting victims of spiritual abuse who thought they were devoted to the highest form of Christianity only to discover they were being used in the name of Christ.

4. Spiritual Parents Have Been Walking in Community and Growing in Intimacy with God Long Enough to Take Others Under Their Wing and Serve as Mentors in the Faith

The apostle Paul once lamented that the Corinthian church had ten thousand guardians but not many fathers (1 Cor. 4:15). He did not mean they had ten thousand people teaching the Bible and nobody was evangelizing (which I have heard people preach). He meant there was a serious lack of mature leaders capable of mentoring others in the faith. His solution was to send them a mature spiritual father capable of modeling the level of maturity needed in the leaders of the church. He sent them someone he had personally discipled. He sent them Timothy.

5. Spiritual Elders Have Functioned as Spiritual Parents for Years (If Not Decades) and Are Ready to Function as Something Like the Elders at the City Gate Often Mentioned in the Old Testament

These elders would gather to discuss the affairs of the city and served as the official judicial system for the area. As the heads of their various families and as those who had successfully raised children to become adults and parents, they had the life experience to bring wisdom to judging the affairs of the city. Such elders were honored and brought a sense of stability to the community.

In the New Testament, the idea of elders in the church is built on this Old Testament idea.[14] Elders were those who had raised their families well, who had decades of life experience, and who were free to give their attention to the affairs of the community and not primarily to their family. While younger men were building the family business and raising their children and preparing them to raise families of their own, elders had completed that part of life and were able to spend their days helping those in need and dealing with problems that arose within the community.

Along with this role of dealing with community problems, elders in the church also served an important role as teachers and intercessors. They were responsible for maintaining orthodox doctrine so that the true gospel was passed on to the next generation and not a perverted gospel—and perversions popped up constantly. They were also responsible for praying for the community and leading the community in prayer.

Elders set the tone for the health of a community. If our elders are immature spiritually and emotionally, our church is in trouble. But when our churches are filled with spiritual parents and elders, there will be a natural flow of raising new generations to a place of spiritual maturity.

LISTENING PRAYER AND EMOTIONAL HEALING

As a pastor, the strategy I employed most often with people who made appointments was listening prayer. My goal was to remove obstacles that might keep people from being able to hear directly from the Spirit in a way that would have an impact I could never have just with the advice I might give, no matter how biblical that advice might be. For example, Connie came to see me because her relationships kept failing and she wondered if there was something wrong with her.[15] I listened to her story then explained the WLVS model described in the chapter on beliefs. She asked God, "Is there a core wound from my past that needs to be healed?" The first memory that came to mind was the day her dad left the house when her parents divorced.

She was tempted to dismiss the memory. After all, most of her friends came from broken homes. She had been told by many good Christian counselors in the past that she simply needed to forgive her parents and replace her thoughts of worthlessness with true statements about her identity in Christ. That was all good advice and true as far as it went. However, it didn't really fix the brokenness inside.

She finally agreed to focus on that memory and began to relive the pain of seeing her dad walking out the door as she sat on the couch. She was only four.

Next, she asked God, "Did the devil succeed in planting any lies in my heart because of this wound?" Immediately two thoughts came to her mind, and I wrote them down: (1) the divorce was your fault, and (2) your dad left because you are unlovable.

We then followed Karl Payne's warfare prayer process—which I will explain more in the next chapter—and she said, "I confess that I have agreed with these lies. I renounce them in Jesus' name and cancel any permission the enemy has in my life because of them." When she started to command the enemy to leave, she couldn't finish the sentence. She said, "In the name of Jesus, I . . ." and she would get stuck. I was able to bind the spirits that were keeping her from finishing her prayer and, with a great sigh of relief, she finished commanding them to leave. I could see her physically relax and she said she felt like a giant weight had been lifted from her shoulders.

At that point, she asked God what the truth was He wanted her to know, and the thoughts that came to her mind were clear and profound:

1. "It wasn't your fault. Your dad just had issues." She had been told this a hundred times, but for the first time it felt true.
2. "You are My delight. You couldn't be more lovable. That is not why your parents divorced."

Again, any Christian counselor could have told her those things, but it would not have had the same weight as knowing it was coming from God. That day she broke a stronghold and started building a new foundation for her life based on truth. Without listening prayer, her breakthrough never would have happened.

DISCERNMENT

Whenever we are paying attention to thoughts and pictures in our mind, we need discernment. Some thoughts come from us. Some come from the enemy. And some come from God. The key is discernment. So, let me give you a few tips on how to discern the differences among the thoughts that run through your mind.

1. Thoughts That Are in Alignment with God Always Promote the Fruit of the Spirit

If thoughts come to me that make me hate someone instead of love them, or rob me of peace and joy rather than promoting my peace and joy, or encourage a lack of self-discipline, then I can be sure that thought is not from God. The devil is not in the habit of promoting the fruit of the Spirit.

2. Thoughts That Are in Alignment with God Make the Truth Feel True

It may seem odd to talk about truth feeling true, but we all know there is a difference between believing something is true in our mind and believing it is true in our heart. At times, we all struggle to feel like God is good, even though our minds know it is true. We struggle to believe we are loved, even though our minds tell us God loves us. So, if I have two thoughts in my head and one says, *You are worthless*, and reminds me of all the times people have made me feel that way (thus, providing evidence that it is true), I can be sure that is from the devil because it is unscriptural. It does not produce the fruit of the Spirit to embrace that thought. On the other hand, if I hear the thought, *You are My delight*, I can be sure that is God because it produces joy and peace and it is scriptural.

The devil often tries to rob us of the "God thoughts" that could give us life. I know many times I have had the thought, *You are a delight to Me*, and immediately felt a compulsion to reject the thought and focus on my failures and inadequacies. So, where do you think that compulsion comes from? It is either the devil or the flesh. Even if it is just the flesh, it is in league with the devil and needs to be rejected.

3. Thoughts That Are in Alignment with God Give Guidance That Bring Hope

As we have seen, hope is directly related to having a plan. It is not unlike God to give us a one- or two-step plan that gives us some hope that all is not lost. For example, I have often had a surprising idea come to mind while preaching or counseling or praying that gave me guidance or insight that I need. More than once I have had someone approach me after a sermon to tell me something I said was "just for them" and recognized that it was the surprising thought that had come to me as I was preaching.

In a similar way, when meeting with people for prayer and counseling, it is not uncommon to have a random thought come to mind that turns out to be the key to the whole situation. The fruit of acting on such thoughts shows that God was behind them.

THE VOICE OF GOD

It should be of no surprise that learning to recognize God's voice plays a significant role in emotional healing. Our God is close to the brokenhearted, and He is a God who heals. As Christians, one of the great advantages we have when it comes to emotional healing is that we are not limited to the physical engines of body, beliefs, and bonding. We have access to God Himself. Through His Spirit, we have access to a personal relationship, wisdom from above, and a God who is powerful. As we will see in the next chapter, we also have authority over wicked spirits that enables us to tear down strongholds and experience a victory the world cannot know.

CHAPTER 10

DELIVER FROM DEMONS

MY INTRODUCTION to spiritual warfare began at age seven. I was home one evening with one of my sisters and a babysitter when I looked in the next room and saw a black-robed, red-eyed creature staring at me. No one else could see it, but it was very tangible to me. I started to scream and the poor people with me must have been beside themselves with shock. As soon as my parents stepped in the front door, the creature left.

That night my dad taught me my first lesson in spiritual warfare. He said, "If anything like that ever shows up again, ask God to cover you with the blood of Jesus then command it to leave in Jesus' name." Several days later, I had a chance to practice. The same creature showed up in my bedroom. This time I prayed, "Lord Jesus, cover me with Your blood," and I commanded it to leave, which it did before I even finished the sentence. It was very comforting to know I could make these things leave that quickly. I never had to deal with anything like it again.

It turns out my mom and dad had helped a woman find freedom

from an oppressive spirit the week before. It was the first time they had done something like that—but I'll tell their story later. The demon I saw had shown up not just to scare me but to intimidate my parents. It was basically a threat, as if it was saying, "Are you sure you want to do this?" The good news is that my parents were smart enough to know you don't make deals with the devil. If you shake hands with the devil and say, "I'll leave you alone, if you leave me alone," that is a deal he will make every time, because he has no intention of keeping his word. It offers no safety to avoid antagonizing the enemy, because if our warfare strategy is avoidance, we are basically admitting we do not believe we have access to a power greater than his.

When I was in college, my theology professor said he rarely taught on demonology, because whenever he did, weird things happened around his home. I thought such thinking was completely backward. If we have an enemy who wants to take us out, how does it make any sense to ignore him and remain completely ignorant of his schemes? Is it not much better to learn how to fight and win spiritual battles? Shouldn't a theology professor be equipping us for battle?

HOW WARFARE WORKS

Every great military commander knows that warfare is deception. Misleading your enemy is of crucial importance to winning battles. During World War II, both sides went to great lengths to deceive their opponents. Before the famous D-Day invasion, the Allies went so far as to create a fictional army supposedly commanded by their most famous commander, George Patton.[1]

Even God keeps the devil guessing what His next step will be in the war of redemption in which we are still enmeshed. The demons could not figure out why Jesus was on earth in human form. They asked Him, "Have you come here to torment us before the time?" (Matt. 8:29 ESV). Paul wrote, "If they had [known], they would not have crucified the Lord of glory" (1 Cor. 2:8), which implies that even the kingdom of darkness might have employed a different strategy if they had known what God was really up to.

At the heart of spiritual warfare, there is also deception. Satan is the father of lies (John 8:44), who masquerades as an angel of light (2 Cor. 11:14) to deceive us in order to enslave us. Just like a hunter uses bait to deceive his prey into entering a trap, so the devil seduces, intimidates, and misleads us in the hope that we will fall into one of his traps.

WHAT DEMONS CAN AND CANNOT DO

Most people I have met are not sure of what demons really are or what exactly they do. To put it simply I think of them as the soldiers whose allegiance is to the kingdom of darkness. In the New Testament, we read of demons affecting our bodies, minds, and emotions.

Bodies

Here are a few examples of demons affecting our bodies. A woman was bent over because of a demonic presence and healed when the spirit was evicted (Luke 13:10–17). We see this with a man who was blind and mute (Matt. 12:22), and a boy who was seized by the compulsion to throw himself into fire or water (Mark 9:22). According to one study, out of thirty-five miracles performed by Jesus, seven of them involved casting out demons.[2]

Mind

As "the father of lies" (John 8:44), the devil is clearly involved in deception. Paul warned the Corinthians that their minds could be led astray by the enemy (2 Cor. 11:3).

Emotions

The Scriptures also portray wicked spirits as able to cause emotional or psychological torment. For example, King Saul was tormented by a demonic spirit (1 Sam. 16:14, 23), and in His parable of the unforgiving servant, Jesus compared the consequences of unforgiveness to being handed over for torment (Matt. 18:32–35). Torment is a good description of the emotional distress many describe when they find themselves battling demonic voices.

WHAT CAN DEMONS DO TO CHRISTIANS?

As Christians, we all know there are consequences for sin. One of those consequences is that demons get greater access to our lives. Some people get stuck on the question: *Can Christians be possessed?* From my perspective, that is not the right question. The question is: *Can Christians give demons access?* I think the answer to the possession question is no. But the answer to the access question is yes. Possession implies ownership, and we are owned by Christ and purchased by His blood. However, access is clearly a possibility. Consider these two Scriptures:

1. **First Corinthians 10:14–22.** Christians can have fellowship (*koinonia*) with demons. In this passage, Paul is addressing the problem of Christians who attend pagan ceremonies and eat the food sacrificed to the idols. He argues that these sacrifices are offered to demons and, thus, Christians who participate in such occult activities are having fellowship with demons. Whatever it means to have fellowship with demons, it certainly sounds like Christians can do things that open the door to demonic activity in their lives.

2. **Ephesians 4:26–27.** Paul warns Christians who let the sun go down on their wrath that one of the consequences is giving the devil a foothold (or a place) in their lives. One of the consequences of sin is permission for the enemy to have access to us.

Sometimes it is argued that the Holy Spirit and demons cannot dwell in the same person. But the Bible never says this. In fact, in the book of Ezekiel, we get a pretty clear picture of how this could happen.

Before Israel went into exile, the Glory of Yahweh (His presence) was residing in the holy of holies at the same time that wicked spirits were being invited into the outer courts. According to Deuteronomy 32:17, the gods of the nations are demons. Thus, when we see that the seventy elders of Israel were worshiping pagan gods in the outer court of the temple (Ezek. 8:11–12) and women were worshiping the Baylonian god Tammuz (Ezek. 8:14), while still others were worshiping the sun (Ezek. 8:16), we get a pretty clear picture of how demons and the Spirit of God could be in the temple at the same time. It is the same with Christians. We are God's temple. The Spirit lives in our hearts, but that does not mean wicked spirits cannot get access to our minds and our bodies.

A witch doctor in the Amazon jungle was led to Christ by a group of missionaries who did not understand spiritual warfare. After his conversion, the witch doctor gave his testimony. You can watch it on YouTube.[3]

According to this shaman, he had invited many spirits to "live inside my chest."[4] He felt he knew the difference between good spirits and bad spirits, but when he met the missionaries he saw something he had never seen before. They had a bright light glowing from inside their chests (it was the Holy Spirit). When the shaman finally gave his life to Christ, the bright light moved into his chest also. However, it didn't automatically evict the other spirits.

As a result, a war broke out. You might say that all hell broke loose because he now had a battle going on inside because the demons didn't want to leave or relinquish control. The missionaries didn't understand any of this and were not equipped to help him evict the wicked spirits, so the shaman did it himself. He went into the jungle and, with the help of Jesus, he came back free from the battle.

The point here is simply this: Christians do not have immunity to demonic activity simply because they are Christians. We must learn to fight. Thus, we put on the armor. We stand. We resist. We wrestle. The advantage of the Christian—and it is immense—is that we don't have to put up with the torment. We have authority in Christ to deal with demonic activity and make it leave.

PERMISSION—HOW WE OPEN DOORS TO THE ENEMY

There are two essential principles for understanding spiritual warfare: permission and authority. If you think of this from a legal perspective, demons need permission to do what they do. Governments can give demons permission to greater activity in their territory when those governments worship pagan gods or endorse sin. Institutions (like schools, businesses, and churches) can give permission to demons to have access to what they do when they enter into agreements with them. For example, I read an article from the BBC that reported hundreds of cases of businesses in Uganda paying to have human sacrifices performed on their property as a means of calling down curses on their competitors and granting them power for victory in their competition for money.[5] Do we really think a business can do something like this without any spiritual consequences?

The principle of permission is especially important in working with individuals because we need to understand the sorts of activities that give demons permission to a place in our lives. I once gave a talk to a group of high school students called, "How to Make the Devil Your Roommate." The premise was simple. We open doors to demonic activity when we do not deal with sin. I often use the acronym SOUL-L to teach a simple model for identifying some of the most common ways this happens.[6]

S—Sin

When we sin but fail to repent of that sin, we open a door to the enemy. Too often, instead of repenting, we justify our sin or simply hide it. This opens a door to demonic activity by giving permission for demons to occupy a place in our lives.

O—Occult

When we sin by direct participation with demons (perhaps by attending a seance or joining a coven), it opens an even bigger door to demonic activity in my life. Whether I am a Christian or not, there are consequences to activity like this. It gives access to demons they wouldn't have if I had not participated in occult experiences.

U—Unforgiveness

When we sin by holding on to our bitterness instead of forgiving those who wrong us, it gives permission to the enemy to torment us at some level. More than one spiritual warfare leader has suggested that unforgiveness is the most common cause of demonization in the church.

L—Lies We Believe

Since the devil is the father of lies, whenever we agree with his lies, we are entering into a kind of pact with him. In a sense, we are saying, "Satan, you are right. God, You are wrong." This type of agreement gives permission to the enemy to a place in our lives. I have seen this quite a bit with self-hatred, fear rooted in lies about the future, and shame.

One of the fastest growing problems in the world today is fear. In most cases, this fear is related to lies we believe. Dealing with oppressive fear often requires renouncing the lies involved and evicting the demons who are using the fear to torment us.

L—Lineage

If our family opened a door to demons in the past and no one ever made them leave, they still have permission to impact the family in future generations. The idea of sin having consequences for future generations is actually a fairly common biblical theme. For example, the Torah forbids Ammonites and Moabites from entering the tabernacle for ten generations (Deut. 23:3). Jesus said His generation would bear the consequences of prior generations (Matt. 12:41–42; 23:36). The Bible has many examples like this. Clearly, there are generational consequences for sin. One of those consequences is greater access to family members.

AUTHORITY—HOW WE EVICT THE ENEMY

Every Christian has authority over demons. It is not a gift given to a few. We have authority in the name of Jesus because we are God's children and because we are seated with Christ in the heavenly realms (Eph. 2:6).

I remember meeting with a woman who had developed psychic abilities after a Hindu guru touched her forehead during a yoga class. She renounced her participation in something that opened a door to the devil and was about to command the wicked spirits to leave when she asked, "Can I really do this? Shouldn't I just pray for Jesus to do it?"

I told her that it was certainly okay to pray, but that in my experience, Jesus rarely did for us what He already gave us the authority to do in His name. I then showed her a chart that demonstrated how being seated with Christ put us in a position above demonic powers. We don't beg them to leave us alone or treat them like superiors. We speak to them from a position of authority as those who are above them. She then commanded the spirits to leave in the name of Jesus and immediately felt lighter. I met with her several months later and she said her psychic abilities had ended that day. She also felt less depression than she had before that appointment.

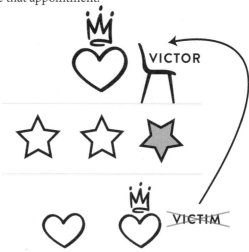

When it comes to using our authority in Christ, there are three core activities mentioned in the Bible.

1. Binding

When we bind spirits, we limit their activity. This is pictured in the words of Jesus when He talks about tying up a strong man before you can rob his house (Matt. 12:28–29). Binding is often done while demons still have permission to be someplace. For example, people sometimes get demonic interference as they are trying to process information. I have seen people fall asleep in mid-sentence, watched their eyes roll back in their heads, or glaze over. I've also seen them simply unable to maintain their train of thought for no apparent reason. For many, they only experience this type of interference when they start to pray, read the Bible, or listen to praise music. In such moments, binding the enemy from creating this interference is a helpful tool. It is usually done with a simple command like this one, "In the name of Jesus, I bind you and command you to stop interfering."

2. Loosing

The idea of loosing suggests untying someone who is in bondage. In Luke 13:16, Jesus refers to His eviction of a wicked spirit from a woman as "loosing" her. In modern language, I think of loosing as canceling permission. Thus, when I forgive someone, I loose myself from the bondage of bitterness. When I repent of a sin, I loose myself from the demonic claim that comes from it. When I renounce a lie, I loose myself from the slavery created by deception. By forgiving, repenting, and renouncing, I loose myself from demonic claims against me. Many times, this is all that is needed in order to experience victory over the enemy. We don't always have to evict wicked spirits, especially if there are no other signs of demonization. Most of the time forgiving, repenting, and renouncing are all that is needed.

3. Evicting

When it comes to evicting wicked spirits, the most common mistake people make is relying solely upon authority instead of dealing with issues of permission first. Evicting a spirit that has permission to be someplace falls into the category of a miracle. It can happen, but it is not the normal legal process. The process I am describing here emphasizes removing any legal claim the enemy has (i.e., its permission), before using our legal authority to remove that spirit. I think of removing the permission as the work of a lawyer and the exercise of authority the work of a police officer. One deals with legal work in court that removes permission. The other enforces the legal work that has been done.

Dr. Karl Payne has put these legal practices together in a simple pattern that can be remembered with three C's:

1. **Confess.** Admit whatever gave permission to the enemy in the first place. This is usually something from the SOUL-L list. This doesn't have to be a long, drawn out prayer. It is usually sufficient to say, "I confess that I participated in the occult." Sometimes it is necessary to be more specific, but not always.

2. **Cancel.** Choose to forgive, repent, or renounce in order to loose yourself from whatever claim the enemy has on you. You can think of this as tearing up the agreement that has given them permission to a place in your life.

3. **Command.** The actual eviction takes place after the permission has been removed. This is also a pretty straightforward process. I may say, "In the name of Jesus, I command every spirit that has taken advantage of my sin to leave." Experience has led many people to add more elements to the eviction statement or process. It can be necessary to get more detailed in more complicated situations.[7]

Here are a few additional commands that often go with eviction.

These additional commands are largely based on experience. Many people who have dealt with demons through the years have found that the enemy often tries to find loopholes to keep some level of permission to stay engaged. People like Mark Bubeck and Karl Payne have developed extensive prayers to close these loopholes.[8] Here are a few common examples:

1. "I bind you all together as one and command that you all leave as one with no one left behind."
2. "I command you to take all of your works and effects with you." In other words, if they have built a stronghold in the person's life, they need to tear it down and take it with them.
3. "I command that no spirits will come to replace the ones who are leaving and that you will truly leave and go where the Lord Jesus sends you. No hiding allowed."
4. Some people send demons to the pit. I usually send them wherever the Lord Jesus Christ tells them to go.

Depending on their training and experience, different ministries may add other elements to the process of confessing, canceling, and commanding.

NOT ALL WARFARE MINISTRIES ARE CREATED EQUAL

If you have never engaged in spiritual warfare ministry before, this may seem a bit overwhelming. My goal is to lay out a few basics like understanding permission and authority and to offer some guidance to those who are already engaged in this sort of ministry and need some help.

I am well aware that many people have gone through deliverance or some form of spiritual warfare ministry and been traumatized by the experience. We could collect a long list of stories of people who came to someone for this type of help and left worse than they came. This shouldn't be surprising. We could say that about virtually every kind of ministry. There are people who go to Bible studies and end up experiencing spiritual abuse, but this doesn't mean attending Bible studies is bad. There are people who study the Bible diligently and end up in heresy. This doesn't mean studying the Bible is bad. In the same way, we need to be careful not to throw out all spiritual warfare ministry just because it is not always done well.

If you go back to the early days of the church, spiritual warfare ministry was core to who the church was. Tertullian wrote that everywhere Christians went, they cast out demons.[9] One of the earliest discipleship manuals ever discovered (the *Didache*), makes deliverance a standard part of the discipleship process.[10] This makes a lot of sense when you stop to think that most Gentiles converting to Christianity were coming out of paganism and would have engaged in a lot of occult activity. Renouncing the devil and breaking agreements that empowered the enemy was standard practice in that culture. It is still standard practice in churches around the world. In my experience, it is only in our Western churches that we seem to struggle to see the necessity of warfare training for every believer. When I travel overseas to speak, I can often skip the usual defense of the idea that Christians can be impacted by demons. They know that happens. What they want to know is how to overcome it.

SPIRITUAL WARFARE: A BIG TOPIC

My goal in this chapter has been to offer help and understanding of the fifth engine that drives our emotions. Spiritual warfare is a big topic, but I hope there has been enough here to help you on your own journey or in ministering to those you are trying to help.

In the final chapter, I will attempt to put everything together to show how the BUILD maturity model provides a holistic, integrated approach to freedom, healing, and wholeness that can bring us hope and direction as we seek breakthrough for ourselves and others.

CHAPTER 11

PUTTING IT ALL TOGETHER: BUILD MATURITY

BY NOW, YOU MAY BE wondering what it might look like to put this model together and apply it to an actual breakthrough journey. Let me start with another fictional character. We'll call him Francis. He represents someone with some deep issues that are not going to resolve quickly. The elements of the story combine to form a picture of the classic person who has lots of A trauma and B trauma that combine to form some deep issues.

Francis grew up in a home with an angry, alcoholic father and an overwhelmed, emotionally unavailable mother. He developed a lot of bad habits as a boy because he was basically parenting himself. But his mother took him to a small Pentecostal church every week that believed God would heal all physical and emotional problems if someone had enough faith. Francis routinely went forward for prayer ministry after the service, and more than once a group of people attempted to evict the spirits of anger and despair that seemed to plague him. Unfortunately, the way they went about it left him more traumatized than helped.

Eventually, the family switched churches and went to a more Bible-focused church. An older man there took an interest in Francis and offered to meet on a regular basis. However, instead of being a spiritual mentor and surrogate father to him, he groomed Francis and began to sexually abuse him. You can imagine the damage this did to the young man's view of God. Not only was his abuser a leader in the church, he often wove Scripture into his justifications for what he did.

By the time he was seventeen, Francis was a lost soul. He was good looking and could be charming, so he had his pick of pretty girls. He was also addicted to alcohol, meth, cigarettes, and porn. He had enormous mood swings and could be incredibly sensitive and cruelly abusive in a single conversation. A few years later, he married the prettiest girl in school and quickly had two kids. They went to church every Sunday, but behind closed doors the cycle of pain and abuse never stopped.

Francis also developed a secret life in which he went to the gay bar in town and sometimes dressed like a girl. The volcano raging below the surface from the sexual abuse he had endured and the lack of emotional capacity from years of neglect had left him completely incapable of functioning as either a husband or a father. He was a broken, angry, confused man. When his marriage inevitably fell apart, Francis had no idea where to turn for help.

Some of you can identify with this story. Elements of it feel all too familiar. Others know someone like this—a person with deep wounds and deep issues that seems beyond help. Let's explore what putting the BUILD maturity model into practice might look like for Francis.

BUILD MATURITY

If Francis had walked into my office when I was a pastor and regularly meeting with people who needed help, I normally had three goals:

1. Listen to his story and make sure he felt heard and seen.

2. Do prayer ministry with him either related to listening prayer, defeating demons, or both.

3. Put together a plan for the next step.

Notice this is not a comprehensive plan for everything that needs to be done. It is just getting a next step in place. Depending on his capacity, I might suggest taking a next step related to each of the five strategies. Here is an example:

1. Body:
   - Start practicing Box Breathing three times a day.
   - Visit a doctor.
   - Join a gym.
   - Start an appreciation journal.
   - Follow a program like the 28 Days to Joy Challenge at 4Habits.org.[1]

2. Beliefs:
   - Read a book like *Taking Every Thought Captive*,[2] *Victory Over the Darkness*,[3] or my book *A Deeper Walk*.[4]
   - Start a daily Bible reading program.
   - Create a T-bar chart for each negative emotion being battled (like shame, anger, fear, disgust, despair, or sadness).
   - Start a journal to track beliefs that suck joy. In the journal, ask Jesus for replacement thoughts that lead to life.

3. Bonding:
   - Find a way to share joy with three people during the week. If necessary, make a list of people and do something small to make them smile.
   - Join a group offered at the church or an online community that will reinforce the healing journey.
   - Write a letter of gratitude to someone.

- Begin to track how often fear is a motivator, and look for joy motivations to replace it.

4. Spirit:
  - Journal about sessions and ask God if there is any truth He wants to reveal.
  - Meet with a prayer minister online or in person.
  - Journal about thought life. Pay attention to thoughts that promote the fruit of the Spirit and thoughts that attack them.
  - Practice daily gratitude. Tell Jesus things to be grateful for and pay attention to the thoughts that follow.
  - Read a book on walking in the Spirit like *Toward A Deeper Walk*[5] or *Experiencing God.*[6]

5. Wicked Spirits:
  - Cleanse home and pray for a hedge of protection each night.
  - Go through *The Steps to Freedom in Christ*[7] with someone online or in person.
  - Practice offensive praying. Ask God to launch an attack against the oppressive spirits.
  - Read a book on spiritual warfare like *What Every Believer Should Know About Spiritual Warfare* or *Spiritual Warfare: Christians, Demonization, and Deliverance.*[8]

This is just a list of options I would use to get Francis or someone like him started. You may know of other practices or resources that would be helpful. The point of a model like BUILD is to have categories for creating a plan either for yourself or for someone you are trying to assist.

WHAT IF RESOURCES ARE MISSING?

Probably the single biggest problem I hear from people looking for help on their journey is that they don't know where to find help with one or more of these strategies. They don't know anyone who does listening prayer or spiritual warfare, or they can't find a group to join. Some can't even find good biblical counseling. One of the reasons I am writing this book is to try to cast a vision for churches to think in terms of building out the networks needed for this kind of ministry. In an ideal world, churches individually or collectively would be able to offer help related to all five strategies of the BUILD maturity model.

For those who can't afford to wait until churches do this, there are online options people can investigate. At Deeper Walk International, we try to provide links to partner ministries and networks who do this kind of work. Of course, the problem with providing links is that you can't guarantee that everyone you list is credible. People still need to do their due diligence, but we try to give people a place to start. Having said this, we still get emails every week from people who thank us for the difference a prayer minister has made in their lives.

DOES THIS WORK?

A few years ago, I told a friend of mine that I had done a talk for a corporation in which I mentioned his wife as an example of a mature person who suffered well. My friend teared up. He had been through hell and back with his wife. Years before, she had been diagnosed with a significant personality disorder. She had almost no emotional capacity and turned into a different person with every emotion she felt. Their marriage had been rocky, and he often wondered if there really was any hope of transformation. To think that she had come so far that she was now held up as someone's ideal for maturity and emotional capacity was almost too much to take in.

Toward the end of her life, my friend's wife found herself in a cancer ward during the pandemic lockdown. She was isolated with virtually no visitors. But she had learned not only how to live with joy and practice appreciation herself, she had also taken it upon herself to be a joy spreader for everyone in the hospital. The more people she was able to help experience joy, the more her own joy increased. The more her joy increased, the more emotional capacity she had to deal with hard stuff like chemotherapy and being isolated from her family.

Another woman who was diagnosed with dissociative identity disorder after being tortured repeatedly as a child has been able to successfully raise a family of her own. It hasn't been easy, but she came to live a pretty normal life and become a source of hope to others.

One woman stopped me at a conference to let me know that thanks to what she had learned from our ministry and the people with whom she had connected, she was alive, sane, and thriving.

Stories have come in from all around the world of people who have discovered the elements of this model. We have stories from Central America, Latin America, Africa, Asia, Europe, India, Australia, New Zealand, Canada, and nearly every state in the union. Most of them just want to say thank you. For many, it is the first time they have heard everything brought together in one place. They normally have to go to one ministry for one strategy and hope to stumble upon the other things they need somewhere else. The integrated model presented in this book has helped them understand their journey much more clearly and given them a better picture of the holes that still need to be filled as they move forward.

My prayer for you is that you will feel encouraged. I know there is a lot of content in a book like this, but the point is that hope is real and there are strategies that work. I pray that something in this book will help you find the breakthrough you need.

One final thought. Our journeys to freedom, healing, and wholeness often have seasons. You may be in a season in which the focus is warfare, walking in the Spirit, or dealing with one of the other engines. You don't have to do everything at once, and you don't have to do everything perfectly. In the end, God is the architect of each one of our journeys. He has a plan for you, and He knows the next step you need and the step after that and the step after that. As Paul wrote, "He who began a good work in you will carry it on to completion until the day of Christ Jesus" (Phil. 1:6).

ACKNOWLEDGMENTS

I WANT TO THANK the many people who have influenced my approach to helping others. Dr. Neil T. Anderson worked closely with my father, Dr. Timothy M. Warner, for many years and taught me the importance of identity in Christ and the simplicity with which spiritual warfare ministry can be explained. Dr. Karl I. Payne is a great friend whose approach to warfare ministry has taken many complicated ideas and made them simple and transferable. Dr. E. James Wilder is also a good friend who has been very generous with his content. I have learned so much from him that his ideas bleed through almost everything I write.

As with any book, there are many I could acknowledge, but let me highlight three people from my staff without whom this book would not have happened. Duane Sherman, Nik Harrang, and my daughter, Stephanie Warner, all proofed this manuscript and made excellent suggestions for improving it. From the Moody team, I also want to thank Drew Dyck for his excellent input and enthusiasm for the project. I especially want to thank Ashleigh Slater for going above and beyond the call to improve this book and help it flow.

NOTES

INTRODUCTION

1. Timothy M. Warner, *Spiritual Warfare: Victory over the Powers of This Dark World* (Wheaton, IL: Crossway, 1991).

2. Neil T. Anderson and Timothy M. Warner, *The Essential Guide to Spiritual Warfare: Learn to Use Spiritual Weapons; Keep Your Mind and Heart Strong in Christ; Recognize Satan's Lies and Defend Your Loved Ones* (Bloomington, MN: Bethany House, 2016). This book was originally published as *The Beginner's Guide to Spiritual Warfare: Using Your Spiritual Weapons, Defending Your Family, Recognizing Satan's Lies* (Ann Arbor, MI: Servant Publications, 2000).

3. The DID diagnoses came from professionals. For more on this specific issue, see my short book for biblical counselors, *A DID Primer: An Introduction to Dissociative Identity Disorder and the Healing Journey* (Carmel, IN: Deeper Walk International, 2010/2019).

4. Story first shared in Marcus Warner, *A Deeper Walk: A Proven Path for Developing a More Vibrant Faith* (Chicago: Moody Publishers, 2022), 75–77.

5. Story first shared in Marcus Warner and Chris Coursey, *The 4 Habits of Joy-Filled People: 15-Minute Brain Science Hacks to a More Connected and Satisfying Life* (Chicago: Northfield Publishing, 2023), 28–29.

6. Perry Noble, "Should Christians Take Medication for Mental Illness?," *Perry Noble* (blog), February 24, 2014, http://perrynoble.com/blog /should-christians-take-medication-for-mental-illness.

7. Dan Rumberger, "Understanding Dissociation" (Restoring the Shattered: A Symposium for Those Working with the Trafficked and Abused at Denver Seminary, June 27, 2019).

CHAPTER 1

1. *Passing the Peace After a Crisis* is a Life Model Works publication available at their website at https://shop.lifemodelworks.org/products /passing-the-peace.

2. Marcus Warner and Jim Wilder, *The Solution of Choice: Four Good Ideas That Neutralized Western Christianity* (Carmel, IN: Deeper Walk International, 2018). The content shared in this section is a summary of ideas presented in this book.

3. William Ames, *The Marrow of Theology*, 2nd ed. (Grand Rapids, MI: Baker Books, 1968). According to an article at APuritansMind.com, Ames was quoted in the American colonies more than Luther and Calvin combined. "William Ames (1576–1633)," *A Puritan's Mind*, https://www.apuritansmind.com/puritan-favorites/william-ames /the-marrow-of-theology-online-by-william-ames-1576-1633/. This particular quote is translated into modern English, but the original in Early Modern English can be found in volume 2, chapter two, line 4.

4. For a good summary, see the article: Emrys Westacott, "Nietzsche's Concept of the Will to Power," *ThoughtCo*, January 29, 2019, https://www .thoughtco.com/nietzsches-concept-of-the-will-to-power-2670658.

5. *A Greek-English Lexicon of the New Testament and Other Early Christian Literature*, 3rd ed. (University of Chicago Press: Chicago, 2000), s.v. "teleios."

6. "Lexicon: G5046 *teleios*," Blue Letter Bible, https://www.blueletterbible .org/lexicon/g5046/kjv/tr/0-1/.

7. Marcus Warner and Chris Coursey, *The 4-Habits of Raising Joy-Filled Kids* (Chicago: Northfield Publishers, 2019).

8. Milan and Kay Yerkovic, *How We Love: Discover Your Love Style. Enhance Your Marriage* (Colorado Springs: WaterBrook, 2017), 13.

CHAPTER 2

1. Henry Cloud and John Townsend, *How People Grow: What the Bible Reveals About Personal Growth* (Zondervan: Grand Rapids: MI, 2001).

2. Cloud and Townsend, *How People Grow*, 16.

3. MADtv, season 6, episode 24, directed by Bruce Leddy, aired May 21, 2001, on Fox.

4. Juni Felix, *You Are Worth the Work: Moving Forward from Trauma to Faith* (Colorado Springs: NavPress, 2021).

5. The word "fear" is used over 500 times in the Bible, and according to one blog that researched this, "There are around 150–200 times we are told to not be afraid in the Bible. This meticulous list tops out at 204." See "365 Instances of 'Fear Not' in the Bible," *TriadSkills* (blog), October 9, 2019, https://triadskills.wordpress.com/2019/10/09/365-instances-of-fear-not-in-the-bible/.

6. Cloud and Townsend, *How People Grow*, 16.

7. Ibid., 17.

8. Ibid.

CHAPTER 4

1. James G. Friesen et al., *The Life Model: Living from the Heart Jesus Gave You* (East Peoria, IL: Shepherd's House, Inc., 2004).

2. "Daniel Siegel: Flipping Your Lid," in *The Developing Mind: How Relationships and the Brain Interact to Shape Who We Are*. 3rd ed. (New York: The Guilford Press, 2020).

3. "Daniel Siegel: Flipping Your Lid," *Heart-Mind Online*, https://heartmind online.org/resources/daniel-siegel-flipping-your-lid.

4. In Appendix 1 of Chris M. Coursey, *The Joy Switch: How Your Brain's Secret Circuit Affects Your Relationships and How You Can Activate It* (Chicago: Northfield Publishing, 2021), he references the "bigger brain" concept as something that grew out of Allan Schore's teaching.

5. Marcus Warner and Jim Wilder, *Rare Leadership: 4 Uncommon Habits for Increasing Trust, Joy, and Engagement in the People You Lead* (Chicago: Moody Publishers, 2016), 29–32.

6. Ibid., 34–38.

7. E. James Wilder, *The Complete Guide to Living with Men* (East Peoria, IL: Shepherd's House, Inc., 2004), 146. Brain image reprinted with permission.

8. Allan N. Schore, "Attachment and the Regulation of the Right Brain," *Attachment and Human Development* 2, no. 1 (April 2000): 23–47, https://www.allanschore.com/pdf/SchoreAttachHumDev.pdf. The primary explanation of the role of the right orbital prefrontal cortex as the command center/joy center/identity center of the brain can be found in *Rare Leadership* in a section written by Dr. Jim Wilder. Marcus Warner and Jim Wilder, *Rare Leadership: 4 Uncommon Habits for Increasing Trust, Joy, and Engagement in the People You Lead* (Chicago: Moody Publishers), 70.
9. The nerve that is triggered is the vagus nerve.

CHAPTER 5

1. These two women are composite characters that fit a lot of characteristics of people I have met with.
2. Marcus Warner and Jim Wilder, *Rare Leadership: 4 Uncommon Habits for Increasing Trust, Joy, and Engagement in the People You Lead* (Chicago: Moody Publishers, 2016).
3. Jim Wilder and Ray Woolridge, *Escaping Enemy Mode: How Our Brains Unite or Divide Us* (Chicago: Northfield Publishing, 2022).
4. Marcus Warner and Chris Coursey, *The 4 Habits of Raising Joy-Filled Kids* (Chicago: Northfield Publishing, 2019).
5. Raymond Jones and E. James Wilder, "Catastrophic Failure to Reach Adult Maturity and the Onset of Addictions: Three Factors Leading to Increasingly Severe Difficulties Implications for Faith Communities," 2003, https://dw7l8ihwgi2oi.cloudfront.net/wp-content/uploads/2022/06/Factors-Leading-to-Addictions.pdf.
6. Jim Wilder, personal communication.
7. James G. Friesen et al., *The Life Model: Living from the Heart Jesus Gave You* (East Peoria, IL: Shepherd's House, Inc., 2004).
8. For more detail on what happens at puberty, see Warner and Coursey, *The 4 Habits of Raising Joy-Filled Kids*, 108–18. See also E. James Wilder, *The Complete Guide to Living with Men* (Pasadena, CA: Shepherd's House, Inc: 2004), 104–14.
9. See Ross Campbell and Gary Chapman, *How to Really Love Your Adult Child: Building a Healthy Relationship in a Changing World* (Chicago: Northfield Publishing, 2011).
10. Marcus Warner and Stefanie Hinman, *Building Bounce: How to Grow Emotional Resilience* (Carmel, IN: Deeper Walk International, 2020), 26.

11. Friesen et al., *The Life Model,* 69–75.

12. Marcus Warner and Chris Coursey, *The 4 Habits of Joy-Filled Marriages* (Chicago: Northfield Publishing, 2017), 95–98.

13. Warner and Hinman, *Building Bounce.* Stefanie Hinman owns the trademark on "Building Bounce."

14. This pattern was originally taught by Chris and Jen Coursey in Thrive Training as a 4+ story. In our book, *The 4 Habits of Joy-Filled People,* Chris and I reorganized that process into the STEP pattern found here.

CHAPTER 6

1. Timothy R. Jennings, *Could It Be This Simple? A Biblical Model for Healing the Mind* (Chattanoga, TN: Lenox, 2012).

2. Daniel Amen, "The Most Important Lesson from 83,000 Brain Scans," TEDxOrangeCoast, YouTube, October 16, 2013, https://www.youtube.com/watch?v=esPRsT-lmw8.

3. Ibid., 8:00–8:12.

4. Ibid., 5:25–5:37.

5. The magazine was *Reader's Digest,* but it was from so long ago, that I have not been able to find the exact article.

6. Bessel van der Kolk, *The Body Keeps the Score: Brain, Mind, and Body in the Healing of Trauma* (New York: Penguin Books, 2015).

7. Bessel van der Kolk, "What Is Trauma? The Author of *The Body Keeps the Score* Explains," *Big Think,* YouTube video, September 17, 2021, 0:10–0:29, https://www.youtube.com/watch?v=BJfmfkDQb14.

8. Mike Shreve, "10 Yoga Poses That Offer Worship to Hindu Deities: Much More than Just Physical Exercises," *The True Light Project,* https://www.thetruelight.net/wp/10-yoga-poses-that-offer-worship-to-hindu-deities/.

9. A website that promotes kundalini yoga writes, "Kundalini yoga is a style of yoga that enables us to channel energy from the base of our spine and up into the Sahasrara (crown chakra) through a collection of chanting, meditation, kriya and pranayama. It has been practiced in India since 500 BC and is derived from the lineage of Rāja Yoga." Liz Burns, "The Kundalini Snake: What Does It Represent and What Are Its Powers?," *YogaJala,* April 19, 2023, https://yogajala.com/the-kundalini-snake.

10. Raymond Jones and E. James Wilder write, "Disruption of quiet-together functions is the strongest predictor of mental illness across the lifetime" in the article, "Catastrophic Failure to Reach Adult Maturity and the Onset of Addictions," 8.

11. Most of these practices were developed as Jim Wilder worked with Chris and Jen Coursey to create non-New Age, scientifically sound ways of helping people develop skills that were missing because of a trauma in their lives. These skills are taught in training offered by THRIVEtoday—see ThriveToday.org. The acrostic BEST is an attempt to present some of the simplest and most effective elements of this training.

12. Stefanie Hinman, *Building Bounce with Kids: A Faith Based Trauma-Informed Approach to Building Resilient Kids* (Self-published, Cedar Gate Publishing, 2021).

CHAPTER 7

1. For those who are concerned that this is New Age visualization, I understand the concern. But this is not the kind of visualization that attempts to create reality by picturing the reality we want like we see in *Think and Grow Rich* by Napoleon Hill. Focused imagination is about picturing our bodies performing tasks properly. It is a very different use of imagination.

2. William Backus, *The Hidden Rift with God* (Minneapolis: Bethany House, 1990).

3. Alaine Pakkala, *Laura: A True Story* (Self-published, Christian Publications, 2002).

4. You can read more about this model in my book *Understanding the Wounded Heart*, 2nd ed. (Carmel, IN: Deeper Walk International, 2019). The model also appears briefly in other books I have written.

5. In the online article, "The Power of Mind and the Promise of Placebo," *WRF.org*, https://www.wrf.org/complementary-therapies/power-of-mind-placebo.

CHAPTER 8

1. The Rat Park experiment was headed by Bruce K. Alexander and a team at Simon Frasier University in British Columbia. See P. F. Hadaway et al., "The Effect of Housing and Gender on Preference for Morphine-Sucrose Solutions in Rats," *Psychopharmacology* 66, no. 1 (1979): 87–91.

2. The quote by Dr. Falk is taken from the online article: "The Power of Peers: Who Influences Your Health," *NIH News in Health*, September 2021, https://newsinhealth.nih.gov/2021/09/power-peers.

3. Chuck Swindoll, *Living Above the Level of Mediocrity: A Commitment to Excellence* (Nashville: W Publishing Group, 1989), 225.

4. Marcus Warner and Jim Wilder, *Rare Leadership: 4 Uncommon Habits for Increasing Trust, Joy, and Engagement in the People You Lead* (Chicago: Moody Publishers, 2016).

5. Ibid., 66.

6. Marcus Warner and Jim Wilder, *Rare Leadership in the Workplace* (Chicago: Northfield Publishing, 2021), 37.

7. Warner and Wilder, *Rare Leadership*, 31.

8. Ibid., 91.

9. Karl Lehman, *Outsmarting Yourself: Catching Your Past Invading the Present and What to Do About It* (Libertyville, IL: Joy Books, 2011), 21.

10. James G. Friesen et al., *The Life Model: Living from the Heart Jesus Gave You* (East Peoria, IL: Shepherd's House, Inc., 2004).

11. Maribeth Poole, "Dismissive Danny," *Maribeth's Mind* (blog), April 9, 2019, https://maribethpoole.com/dismissive-Danny/; Maribeth Poole, "Distracted David," *Maribeth's Mind* (blog), July 1, 2019, https://maribethpoole.com/distracted-david/; Maribeth Poole, "Disorganized Debbie," *Maribeth's Mind* (blog), July 25, 2019, https://maribethpoole.com/disorganized-Debbie/.

12. Poole, "Distracted David."

13. Alaine Pakkala, *Taking Every Thought Captive: Spiritual Workouts to Help Renew Your Mind in God's Truth* (Colorado Springs: Lydia Press, 1995).

CHAPTER 9

1. This is a fictional story based on a compilation of people and experiences.

2. More than once, I have had people tell me that Jesus played the role of warrior and defender. In one case, He skewered a demon with a sword. In another case, He forcibly removed an abuser. The point of such experiences seems to be to let the person know they are worth defending. It is also not out of character with Jesus, who made a whip and drove out the buyers and sellers, or with the idea that Yahweh is a warrior (Ex. 15:3) and that Jesus will return some day as a judge covered in blood (Isa. 63:1; Rev. 19:15, 21).

3. A. W. Tozer, *The Pursuit of God* (Savage, MN: Broadstreet Publishing, 2007), 55. Retrieved from https://www.google.com/books/edition/The_Pursuit_of_God/1e-8c5dgujsC?hl=en&gbpv=1.

4. Henry T. Blackaby, Richard Blackaby, and Claude V. King, *Experiencing God: Knowing and Doing the Will of God* (Nashville: B&H Publishing Group, 2021), 56.

5. Charles Haddon Spurgeon, "How to Converse with God," *The Spurgeon Center*, September 19, 1875, https://www.spurgeon.org/resource-library /sermons/how-to-converse-with-god/#flipbook/.

6. An article at CompellingTruth.org titled, "What Is Inner Healing, and Is It Biblical?" offers several warnings similar to those I have mentioned, but in the end affirms that inner healing is primarily about "hearing God's voice." The article says, "Inner healing requires being honest with yourself about your feelings and personal experiences and then taking those things to God, seeking His answers and healing. Sometimes we can arrive at this place of inner healing and freedom on our own through studying God's Word and *listening to His voice*. Other times it is beneficial and necessary to seek additional professional help, such as through a Christian counselor" (italic highlights added): https://www.compelling truth.org/inner-healing.html.

7. Dr. Karl Lehman was in charge of providing prayer ministry for people at the conference who wanted prayer for personal issues. The following is a link to the ministry guidelines that were used: https://www.immanuelap proach.com/wp-content/uploads/2022/11/Urbana-Prayer-Ministry -Handbook.pdf.

8. For one source on this, I recommend Craig S. Keener, *Miracles Today: The Supernatural Work of God in the Modern World* (Grand Rapids, MI: Baker Academic, 2021). He has done extensive research verifying miracles of all sorts across the world.

9. This woman's story is also found in this video: "Suicidal Iranian Mother and Daughter Found the Answer of Cure," MuslimTestimony.com, YouTube, July 28, 2013, https://www.youtube.com/watch?v=6dLiSFn71_Q.

10. See her video testimony: "Incredible Story of How 2 Iranian Muslim Women Found Jesus," Road2Jesus, YouTube, January 18, 2015, https:// www.youtube.com/watch?v=bkczulZ-LkY.

11. Berserkers may have been on drugs, or they may have been in an emotional frenzy, but they were devoted to the god Odin and a case can be made they were possessed by pagan spirits and thus were extremely strong and almost impervious to pain. "His (Odin's) men rushed forwards without armour, were as mad as dogs or wolves, bit their shields, and were strong as bears or wild oxen, and killed people at a blow, but neither fire nor iron told upon them. This was called *Berserkergang*." Samuel Laing, *The Heimskringla or the Sagas of the Norse Kings* (London: John. C. Nimo, 1889), 276. Cited in Wikipedia.

12. For a sample of doctrinal prayers related to spiritual warfare, see Mark I. Bubeck, *Prayer Patterns for Revival* (Chicago: Moody Publishers, 2020) and Judy Dunagan, *The Loudest Roar: Living in the Unshakable Victory of Christ* (Chicago: Moody Publishers, 2022).

13. This concept is developed in detail in the book *The Other Half of Church: Christian Community, Brain Science, and Overcoming Spiritual Stagnation* by Michel Hendricks and Jim Wilder (Chicago: Moody Publishers, 2021).

14. Encyclopedia of the Bible, "Elder in the NT," https://www.biblegateway.com/resources/encyclopedia-of-the-bible/Elder-NT.

15. Connie is a composite character.

CHAPTER 10

1. Everett Munez, "Operation Fortitude," *Britannica.com*, https://www.britannica.com/event/Operation-Fortitude.

2. Harold Willmington, "What You Need to Know About Jesus' Miracles: Demon Casting," (2007): 34, https://digitalcommons.liberty.edu/will_know/34. (1) Man in a synagogue (Luke 4:33); (2) a blind and mute demoniac (Matt. 12:22); (3) the Gadarene demoniac (Matt. 8:28–34); (4) a deaf and mute demoniac (Mark 9:25); (5) daughter of a Syrophoenician mother (Mark 7:24–30); (6) a boy at the base of Mt. Hermon (Mark 9:22); (7) woman in a synagogue (Luke 13:11).

3. "Chief Shoefoot—'I'll Never Go Back'—Preview," Lighthouse Trails Publishing, YouTube, November 2021, https://www.youtube.com/watch?v=k8gYjBpoJ0s.

4. Ibid., 5:15–5:20.

5. Chris Rogers, "Where Child Sacrifice Is a Business," BBC , October 11, 2011, https://www.bbc.com/news/world-africa-15255357.

6. Marcus Warner, *What Every Believer Should Know About Spiritual Warfare* (Carmel, IN: Deeper Walk International, 2011).

7. Karl Payne, *Spiritual Warfare: Christians, Demonization, and Deliverance*, 2nd ed. (Republic Book Publishers, 2021), 123–44.

8. Payne, *Spiritual Warfare*; Mark Bubeck, *Spiritual Warfare Prayers* (Chicago: Moody, 1997).

9. "Why, all the authority and power we have over [demons] is from our naming the name of Christ, and recalling to their memory the woes with which God threatens them at the hands of Christ as Judge, and which they expect one day to overtake them. Fearing Christ in God, and God

in Christ, they become subject to the servants of God and Christ. So at our touch and breathing, overwhelmed by the thought and realization of those judgment fires, they leave at our command the bodies they have entered, unwilling, and distressed, and before your very eyes put to an open shame." Tertullian, *Apology*, trans. S. Thewall, chap. 23, http://logoslibrary.org/tertullian/apology/23.html.

10. Clinton Arnold, "Early Church Catechesis and New Christians' Classes in Contemporary Evangelicalism," *JETS* 47, no. 1 (March 2004): 39–54, https://www.etsjets.org/files/JETS-PDFs/47/47-1/47-1-pp039-054_JETS.pdf.

CHAPTER 11

1. Marcus Warner and Chris Coursey, "Take the 28 Day Challenge," 4habits.org, https://4habits.org/.

2. Alaine Pakkala, *Taking Every Thought Captive: Spiritual Workouts to Help Renew Your Mind in God's Truth* (Colorado Springs: Lydia Press, 1995).

3. Neil T. Anderson, *Victory over the Darkness: Realize the Power of Your Identity in Christ* (Minneapolis: Bethany House, 2020).

4. Marcus Warner, *A Deeper Walk: A Proven Path for Developing a More Vibrant Faith* (Chicago: Moody Publishers, 2022).

5. Marcus Warner, *Toward A Deeper Walk* (Carmel: IN, Deeper Walk International, 2006).

6. Henry T. Blackaby, Ricard Blackary, and Claude V. King, *Experiencing God: Knowing and Doing the Will of God* (Nashville: B&H Publishing Group, 2021).

7. Neil T. Anderson, *The Steps to Freedom in Christ: A Biblical Guide to Help You Resolve Personal and Spiritual Conflicts and Become a Fruitful Disciple of Jesus* (Minneapolis: Bethany House Publishers, 2017).

8. Karl Payne, *Spiritual Warfare: Christians, Demonization, and Deliverance*, 2nd ed. (Republic Book Publishers, 2021).

GO DEEPER WITH JESUS BY BREAKING FREE OF LEFT-BRAINED DISCIPLESHIP.

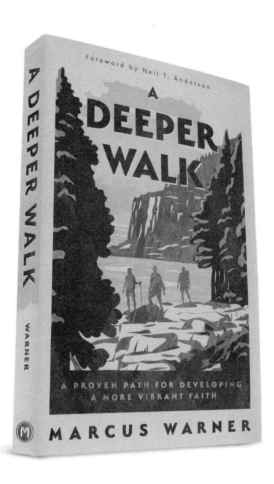

MOODY Publishers

From the Word to Life

Too many Christians are stuck and unable to go deeper in their walk with God because traditional discipleship models are overly left-brained and miss the heart. Warner provides a model for whole-brained, heart-focused discipleship based on the gospel's four essential elements: freedom, identity, spirit, and heart-focused community.

Also available as an eBook and audiobook

Take your next step.

Resources & Training in
Heart-Focused Discipleship

Visit our website today for free resources:
deeperwalkinternational.org.